D1526828

Cathedral Cities of Italy

W. W. COLLINS, R. I.

Originally Published by
William Heinemann
1911

Contents

PREFACE

THE cathedral cities of Italy, the heir of all the ages in art, are as full of enchantment to the lover of architecture as to the poet, the painter, and the historian. Side by side with the great churches that give them their crowning splendour are the public buildings, universities, palaces, and fountains that tell the story of the glorious past, and form the best monument of their great creators. These architectural jewels are often set amidst scenes of great natural beauty, which relieve and enhance the perfection of their art. Every traveller in Italy will recall the emotion with which he first saw Rome rising from the green stretches of the Campagna, recognised the domes and campaniles of Florence, or lifted up his eyes to one of those towered "cities set upon an hill, which cannot be hid"—Siena, Perugia, or Orvieto. Among the many appeals which Italy makes to æsthetic appreciation is that of infinite variety. In no country are the different styles and periods so wonderfully exemplified. Here we may range from Rome and Verona, with their relics of the antique world—amphitheatres, temples, and thermæ—to the Byzantine glories of Ravenna and Venice, the Romanesque grandeur that finds typical expression in the cathedral of Pisa, and thence to the manifestations of that Gothic art which, though it was alien to the climate and character of Italy and so struck no deep roots into the soil, intervened between Romanesque architecture and that of the Renaissance as a brilliant episode, and finds stupendous expression in the thousand pinnacles of Milan.

It is with Christian Italy that we have to deal, the Italy of cathedrals, and it is at Ravenna and at Venice that we may trace the decline of Roman architectural methods and the gradual merging of these into Byzantine forms. Though the great Basilica Ursiana of the fourth century has disappeared, Ravenna has preserved many famous monuments of the fifth century: the votive church of Galla Placidia, sister of the Emperor Honorius, the Baptistery, the aulic church of the Gothic conqueror Theodoric, Sant' Apollinare Nuovo, and the churches of San Vitale and Sant' Apollinare in Classe. Venice, rising to power and splendour when Ravenna fell on evil days, secured the heritage of her glory, and carried on the Byzantine tradition in the cathedral of Torcello, the church of San Zaccaria, and above all in the incomparable San Marco. At Pisa the Romanesque evolution culminated in a

1

unique group of buildings, famous throughout the world, while at Milan and in the surrounding district the local type of Romanesque became sufficiently individual to figure as an independent style under the title of Lombard architecture. Of this subdivision of Romanesque the prototype seems to have been the great church of Sant' Ambrogio at Milan, while San Michele at Pavia is another early and important example. Italy's essays in Gothic are scattered throughout the length and breadth of the peninsula, from Como to Naples. The Broletto at Como and the monastic buildings at Vercelli are said to have inaugurated them. Good examples are the cathedral at Como, the church of San Francesco at Assisi, the cathedral of Orvieto, San Petronio and San Francesco at Bologna, and San Lorenzo at Genoa.

But it is to the Renaissance architecture of Italy that many of us will turn as the most intimate expression of the Italian spirit, to the works of Brunellesco, Michelozzo, and Cronaca at Florence, of Palladio at Venice and Vicenza, of Bramante, and, above all, of Michelangelo at Rome, notably in his great life-work, the church of St. Peter. The exuberant later style that resulted from a too ardent application of the principles of Michelangelo and is known as Baroque, though generally reprobated at present, must not be too sweepingly condemned. It had an exponent of great talent in Bernini, and it will hardly be denied that it gave grandiose expression to the tendency of a splendour-loving age, and that Rome owes to its exponents much of the scenic effectiveness of her streets and the impressive magnificence of her interiors.

COMO

ON a flat piece of land at the southern extremity of Italy's most beautiful lake, the ancient Lacus Larius, stands a city whose history dates back to the days when a Grecian colony nestled at the foot of the mountains which lie east and west of the modern Como. Numerous relics of Roman days found at different times, testify to the truth of the younger Pliny's letters that the Comum Novum of Julius Cæsar was in a flourishing condition during the writer's life, and enjoyed all the privileges attached to a *municipium*.

At the present day Como is best known as a starting-point for tourists who board the steamers at the quay and leave their decks at one of the many delightful spots which fringe the shores of a lake whose attractions cannot be overwritten. The sun shines on an endless panorama which changes every minute as the steamer pants over the blue waters, breaking up and dispelling the reflections of verdure-clad slopes and stern crags which lie mirrored on the surface. Hamlets like Nesso cling to the rocks and bridge the *orriao* or torrent, as it enters the lake in a foaming cascade. Monster hotel settlements like Bellagio and Cadenabbia lie further up the water, opposite to Varenna with its golf course and English caravanserai. Little is left to remind one of those bloody sixteenth-century days when Il Medeghino from his stronghold of Musso ruled the lake, and with his fleet of seven big ships and countless smaller craft blockaded the City of Como, held for Charles V. by the Marquis of Pescara, and compelled the Spaniards to come to terms. Nothing more warlike nowadays ruffles the serenity of the waters than the evil-looking little *dogana* craft which flash their light along the shores, sweeping every tiny bay in search of *contrabbandieri*. Though much could be written about the internecine wars the mountains have seen, it is not with Gian Giacomo de' Medici this chapter is concerned, but with the city itself, which lies away out of sight of the great corsair's Castle of Musso.

3

Figure 1: THE BROTELLO AND CATHEDRAL, COMO

THE BROTELLO AND CATHEDRAL, COMO

The Cathedral of Como, built entirely of marble, was commenced in 1396 from the plans of Lorenzi de' Spazi. The west façade, begun in 1460, was finished by Tomaso Rodario in the last few years of that century. It is Italian Gothic, with the exception of the three doorways, which are rich Lombard work; and, like all façades of the same style in Italy, has the appearance of simply facing or being stuck on to the building itself. Despite the adornment of statues and bas-reliefs, scrolls and arabesques, it has a very severe and flat look, which is unrelieved by the recesses containing busts of the two Plinys on either side of the central doorway, or the deep-set windows and canopied niches above. A fine wheel window occupies a position above the principal door and between these is a good Gothic screen with figures in five niches flanked by a couple of windows on either side.

The north side of the façade adjoins the Brotello, through the arches of which one reaches the north doorway. This is decidedly good. The porch is supported by elegant pillars and adorned by arabesques with birds, animals,

and other figures. It was executed from designs by Rodario, and with the
south portal possesses all the merit that good Renaissance work gives to
both. The windows of the aisles are beautifully ornamented with decoration
of the same character, and the slender pinnacles with their pierced galleries,
albeit they remind one in their whiteness of the superior pieces of an ivory
chess set, break the line of the roof in a most agreeable manner. The dome
lacks proportion and is of the over-done style of French eighteenth-century
work.

The interior of the cathedral is Gothic and Renaissance. The nave and
aisles belong to the earlier date. The groining is good, but spoilt, as is
generally found to be the case throughout Italy, by gilded and coloured bosses
which mar the otherwise simple effect of the vaulting. The transepts and choir
are Renaissance, and though the sympathies of the northman are more with
the sterner style, it must be owned that in Como's cathedral the scheme of
decoration found in these is more fitting and better of its sort than in the
Gothic half of the building. At the west end of the nave stands the circular
Baptistery attributed to Bramante, close by which are a lion and lioness, the
former grasping a deer and the latter suckling her young. They support the
two holy water basins. Among the pictures of interest which the cathedral
contains is a good Bernardino Luini of the Virgin, and two glazed and framed
frescoes of the Nativity and Adoration by the same hand.

The illustration shows the Brotello or old town hall, and the pinnacles and
north walls of the Cathedral. The Brotello is faced with banded black and
white marble, the common device for exterior walls in most Italian Gothic
churches, and in this case justified by the beautiful colour it has taken on
with age. The building stands mellowed by the hand of Time, a memorial
of the days of the old Italian Republics; and its counterpart existed in every
Lombard city. Above the arches, under which the good citizens were wont
to discuss the affairs of their town while sauntering to and fro in the cool
shade, is the great hall wherein the chief of the municipality assembled. From
the window in the centre access was obtained to the bar, or *ringhiéra* outside,
from which addresses were delivered to the crowd below, who in constitutional
language formed the *parliamento* and from whom the powers of government
emanated.

Two of the old city gateways still exist, the latter of which, the Porta del
Torre, leading out on the high road to Milan is to-day but an empty five-
storied shell. The old walls may be traced even now on the three sides of the
city away from the water-front. But for these there is very little left to show
the extent of a place which was once a serious rival to Milan. The staple
industry is stone-working, for which the Comaschi have for centuries been
widely known. In former times Como was justly celebrated for the products
of its looms, excelling in number those at Lyons. Nowadays it exports the
raw silk; the looms have sadly fallen off and diminished, and small industries
have taken the place of those that brought considerable wealth to the pockets

of its merchants.

MILAN

WHEN the great wave of conquest which swept mid-Europe in the fifth century broke against the walls of Châlons-sur-Marne and the westward march of Attila and his Huns was checked, the defeated hordes of the East followed their chief across the Alps and invaded the plain that stretches away now, just as it did in those far-off days, to the sunny seas that beat against the southern slopes of the Apennines. In the centre of this plain stood Mediolanum, a city ranking second only to Rome, and her greatest colony in the Peninsula. So rich and prosperous a place became of necessity the object of attack, and the hosts that looked to "the Scourge of God" as leader, swept into and through the fair city, sacking it completely. Rebuilt, but once again undergoing the same fate at the hands of Frederick I. in 1162, there remain but a colonnade of sixteen Corinthian columns near the Porta Ticinese, a few tablets and fragments let into the walls of other gateways, and some relics in the museum, to tell of the past glories of Rome's great colony.

Milan, as we know it now, is the centre of commercial Italy. Intersected by an excellent system of tramways, with beautiful public gardens and magnificent buildings, it is up to date in every way and stands quite apart from all the other cities with which this book is concerned. The one thing that, perhaps, above all others places it in this position is, however, no product of this commercial age, but its world-famous work of art, the great cathedral, through the lofty aisles of which still reverberates the grand music of the Ambrosian Ritual. The exterior of this immense church, next in Italy to St. Peter's in size, is adorned by a forest of spires, pinnacles, turrets and lace-like tracery. In the midst of all this rises the central tower with its airy spire, from the base of which on a clear day the snow-clad peaks of the Alps may be seen stretching miles on miles away, and bounding the whole of the northern horizon by a lovely dreamland of colour.

Very few buildings compel one's admiration as this does, an admiration wrung in my case from a mind out of sympathy with everything that lacks the dignity of repose; but such is the effect obtained by hundreds of pinnacles and statues, by the turreted flying buttresses, by the filling of every available foot of space with ornament, that one cannot but appreciate the result of the skill and patience so truly Italian, which has carried out these infinite details and produced the great work that stands in the Piazza del Duomo. The present fabric, dedicated "Mariæ Nascenti," is the third cathedral built on the site: the first was destroyed by Attila in 452, and the second by Barbarossa in 1162. The foundation-stone was laid in 1387 by Gian' Galeazzo Visconti, who from a northern clime sought his architect, Heinrich Ahrler, of Gmünden. From that time down to the present day many have had a hand in its making, among them Bramante, Leonardo da Vinci, and Giulio Romano, and the wonder is that the great structure is not far more full of incongruities than it is. The whole exterior is built of white marble from the quarries of la Gandoglia on the Simplon Road, given by the founder for this purpose.

The façade rises with a course of open Gothic work to the gable above, and is divided into five sections which terminate in clusters of Gothic turrets surmounted by pinnacles and statues. The central doorway is surrounded by excellent Renaissance sculpture, the door itself being a magnificent piece of seventeenth-century bronze work. On each side are two more portals. The bases of the intervening buttresses contain splendid panels, and the Caryatides, which support the slender Gothic shafts right and left, by Rusca and Carabelli, are extremely good in pose and execution. The great façade designed by Pellegrini for S. Carlo Borromeo in 1560 was never carried out owing to the saint's death while Pellegrini was away in Spain working on the Escorial for Philip II. The east end is the oldest part of the building, and is almost entirely taken up by three grand Gothic windows. The east window, which is of most beautiful tracery, was executed from the designs of a Frenchman, Nicholas Bonaventure. Both the other windows are fine, but the upper portion or rose pattern, although in itself very delicate, appears "stuck in," and not part of the design; some of the glass in these is very rich in colour. The archivolts of the arches are filled with figures which follow the curve in a rather uncomfortable style, not only here but in every other window save the fine classical of the façade.

Figure 2: THE CATHEDRAL, MILAN

THE CATHEDRAL, MILAN

The interior is grand, and of immense height, albeit the vaulting with its admirably painted tracery is evidence of the great skill of the Italian at "faking." The mellow light from the amber coloured glass of the octagon and the twilight filtering through the gorgeous hues of the other windows is remarkably and impressively pleasing. The columns of the nave, in clusters of eight shafts, are eighty feet high, and carry narrow capitals of foliage which form the base to eight canopied niches occupied by figures of saints—a fine feature. The aisles are double, the outside being lower than that next the nave. The four columns at the crossing which support the octagon are of larger dimensions than those in the nave. Two semicircular pulpits covered with bas-reliefs of gilded bronze stand on either side of the steps leading into the choir, to the solemn darkness of which the shadows thrown from the sounding-boards above make pictorially a good foreground introduction. These pulpits are supported by caryatides representing the Evangelists and four doctors of the Church.

The choir was designed by Pellegrini, and contains a fine sixteenth-century tabernacle of gilded bronze. Beneath is the subterranean church, through which one enters the tiny chapel, under the central spire, wherein is deposited, in a magnificent silver shrine the gift of Philip IV. of Spain, the body of S. Carlo Borromeo dressed in full pontificals. Born in 1538 he was created cardinal by his uncle, Pius IV., in 1561. After the close of the Council of

Trent he assisted other prelates to draw up the epitome of Catholic doctrine, the "Catechismus Tridentinus"; but it is more for his good works and great charity, especially during the plague of 1576, that he lives in the hearts of the Milanese.

In the north transept is a very good example of the metal work of the thirteenth century, in the shape of a fine bejewelled bronze candelabrum. It forms a tree and has many quaint figures in its intricate design. In a chapel in this aisle is the old wooden crucifix which S. Carlo carried when barefooted he tramped the streets during the plague, tending the sick. In the south transept close to the corner near the staircase leading on to the roof is a monument to Giacomo and Gabriele de' Medici, brothers of Pius IV., and a bronze statue of S. Bartolommeo which represents him flayed. The south sacristy door is a fine specimen of Gothic work. Unlike the exterior effect, nothing obtrudes inside this great cathedral. The eye on entering looks straight up to the east, conscious as it travels there, of great pillars rising into the gloom of the vault above, of fine glass and restful solemnity, in which even the chapels in the aisles are lost, to be discovered later on only when searched for.

Next to "Mariæ Nascenti," but taking precedence in archæological interest, is the church of S. Ambrogio, a basilica dedicated by the Saint when bishop of Milan in 387 to SS. Gervasius and Protasius. It was enlarged and rebuilt in 881 and restored by Ricchini in 1631, all the original features being faithfully preserved. A closed courtyard stands below the level of the piazza outside and forms the Atrium beyond which no catechumens were allowed to pass. The capitals of the columns here have the tendency of early Christian Art and adaptations of Runic and Byzantine carving. The church is Lombardo Romanesque. Beneath the gallery over the peristyle is the celebrated door, well guarded by an iron grille, some of the cypress-wood panels of which formed portions of the gate of the Basilica Portiana closed by S. Ambrose against the Emperor Theodosius after his cruel slaughter in Thessalonica. The nave is entered by two side doors and is composed of eight bays, the columns of which are slender in proportion for the deep shadows of the dark aisles. Pilasters run up to the low round vaulting, the large galleries over the aisles being divided by these. Up a few steps which cross the nave at the last bay, and behind a low marble balustrade, is the High Altar, enclosed by one of the finest extant relics of the goldsmith's art. This magnificent casing bears the name of its German maker, Wolvinius. Some of the panels, notably that of the Transfiguration, are very Greek in treatment. The back is almost of better workmanship than the front and is more interesting, as Wolvinius has here illustrated the principal events in the life of the founder. The enamelled borders of these silver-gilt panels are of exquisite design. One of the saint as a child asleep in his cradle with a swarm of bees hovering around, considered a presage of future eloquence, is very naïve. The *baldachino* above this altar is borne by four grand columns of black porphyry.

Up twelve steps are the choir and tribune, and at the end of these is the primitive throne of the Archbishop of Milan, known as the chair of S. Ambrose. The eighteen seats occupied by the suffragans of the province no longer exist, having been replaced in the sixteenth century by carved wooden stalls, and thus has perished a feature identical with the Cathedral at Torcello. The semi-domed roof of the Tribune is covered with a fine ninth-century mosaic which represents the seated figure of the Almighty, beneath whom are SS. Candida, Gervasius, Protasius, Marcellina and Satirus, and a representation of the cities of Milan and Tours—Tours because there, when S. Martin was undergoing martyrdom, the spirit of S. Ambrose went to give him strength. Beneath the choir is the crypt, and at its termination, exactly under the high altar in the church above, in a splendid casket of silver and crystal, repose the remains of three Saints, Ambrose, Gervasius and Protasius. There is a curious pulpit in the church of very early Lombard work, with an "Agape" or love feast carved upon its panels. Close by upon a granite pillar rests a bronze serpent, said to be the brazen serpent of the desert and presented to Archbishop Arnulphus by the Emperor of Constantinople. S. Ambrogio was the church in which the Lombard rulers were crowned with the Iron Crown that is the chief attraction in the neighbouring city of Monza.

So well known are the art treasures of Milan that it is hardly necessary to do more than allude to the many works of great interest in the Brera, formerly a Jesuit college, and in the celebrated Biblioteca Ambrosiana; or that greatest wonder of all which has drawn so many pilgrims to the Cenacolo, the refectory near the church of Santa Maria della Grazie—the much restored Last Supper by Leonardo da Vinci. The Castello of Milan was at one time the residence of the great Visconti family, and at the death of the last male representative passed by marriage into the hands of the first duke of the Sforza line. It was during their reign that Milan took the lead in the fashion of Europe (whence we have the word "milliner") and it was then that Leonardo wrought his masterpieces, including that great equestrian statue of Francesco Sforza which was the wonder of Milan, and of which posterity was so unhappily robbed by the French invasion.

PAVIA

FROM its position close to the confluence of the rivers Po and Ticino, Pavia, the "City of a hundred Towers," was for centuries a point of strategic importance. It is at present a great artillery station. Of its hundred towers that stood at intervals around the eleventh-century walls, hardly one remains, and the old fortifications which had been reconstructed at a later date, are rapidly being converted into a spacious and shady boulevard. The celebrated bridge is however still intact, despite many violent floods, a delight to the eye and a pleasant promenade on a hot day. This notable structure, which spans the Ticino, was built by one of the great Visconti family—Gian' Galeozzo—and is roofed in.

Pavia at one time was rich in noble churches. Many have been demolished, others have fallen into decay. The cathedral, dedicated to S. Stefano, stands on the site of one erected in the seventh century. The present edifice was designed by Bramante and constructed under the direction of one of his pupils, Cristoforo Rocci. In the original plan the nave, transepts, and choir were all of one size, but the nave is the only part in which the great architect's measurements were followed. The façade, approached by a good flight of steps, is unfinished. On the north, and adjoining a fine example of a late Romanesque gateway, stands the *campanile*.

The interior of the main building is grey stone which has not been spoilt by the application of the whitewash brush. A fine pulpit, somewhat similar to those at Milan, stands out from one of the massive piers that support the octagon. It is of singularly large dimensions and is supported by well-carved wooden figures of the Fathers of the Church. The octagon, which carries a good dome and tower and is best seen from the market square, rises well above the roofs of the nave and choir. A gallery running round the entire cathedral forms a triforium, broken only by *trasparente* lights in the apse and side chapels of the choir. These windows accentuate the bad points of the *barroque* altars beneath. The clerestory lights are circular. If it were not for the magnificent tomb in which repose the remains of S. Augustine, the greatest of the Fathers of the Latin Church, the cathedral would be, notwithstanding the fame of its designer, the least interesting ecclesiastical building in Pavia.

Figure 3: THE CATHEDRAL, PAVIA

THE CATHEDRAL, PAVIA

Experts disagree as to who was responsible for the fine monument which covers S. Augustine's remains. The body of the saint had been removed from Hippo, a suffragan see of Carthage, to Sardinia during the Arian persecutions. It rested there until Liutprand, the Lombard king, having purchased it, placed it in the church of S. Pietro in Cielo d'Oro; and when this church was destroyed it was conveyed to the cathedral. On certain festivals the silver casket, portions of which are the original, that contains the bones of the saint robed in full pontificals is removed from its usual position and hoisted up behind the tomb, so that the devout can mount a temporary wooden stair and look on all that is left of the great father.

A figure of the saint lies stretched on the sepulchral urn that usually holds the silver casket. This rests on the basement, or lowest, of the four tiers that compose the monument. Around it are figures of the lesser saints of his Order. Above are bas-reliefs of the chief events in his life and the miracles which after his death were performed in different places through his intercessions. The liberal arts, the cardinal virtues, and many symbols adorn the tomb, which is also decorated with statues of saints and angels, two hundred and ninety in all. They are extremely well executed and enhance the beauty of the design.

The church of S. Michele is a primitive structure and bears traces of being the precursor of all ecclesiastical edifices of the Lombard style of architecture. It was originally a basilica, but short transepts have been added and the roof, which is groined, is vaulted with stone. The oldest part of the church is the crypt, which is under the choir. This is probably the building, or part of it, in which Unulfus sought sanctuary in 661 when fleeing from King Grimoladus. Four compound piers in the nave are adorned with an extraordinary series of sphinxes, symbols, animals and other figures. The façade is decorated with reliefs in a richly coloured sandstone, and has a gabled gallery that is continued round the exterior as far as the apse.

The portals are covered with a profusion of very archaic imagery in which Pagan as well as Christian subjects form most of the decoration. Sculptured bands of sandstone are placed in courses along the whole front and medallions let into the walls. These are very massively built of stone, and though restoration is evident throughout the church it still bears the impress of great age.

Sta. Maria del Carmine is a fourteenth-century building of Gothic design, and is one of the very best examples of brickwork in all Italy. The beautiful rose window of the west front and the three pointed doors with their well-moulded terra-cotta ornament could hardly be finer. Seven elegant pinnacles stand on the rather heavy cornice, forming a good set off to the *campanile*, which, surmounted by a brick spire, is a landmark in the district. The brick piers of the interior are exceptionally good; four squares constitute the nave, the arches of each carry simple groining. Two small lancet-shaped arches, out of all proportion with the massive brick piers that support them, open into the aisles. They have double capitals, the upper being of stone, the lower of carved brick.

In the ruined church of S. Pietro in Cielo d'Oro stood the tomb of Boethius, who under Theodoric held high office in the state. Boethius was executed in Pavia after a long and rigorous confinement in the Casa Malsap ina, during which he wrote his incomparable "Consolations of Philosophy." This work was translated into many languages and was one of the most widely known treatises in the Middle Ages. Alfred the Great translated it into Saxon. Another connection with England exists through Archbishop Lanfranc who accompanied William the Conqueror across the sea and was made prelate of Canterbury. The district round Pavia is not healthy, a condition due probably to the intricate system of irrigation by which the pastures are kept green with a rank-growing grass. Between Pavia, Piacenza and Lodi—a triangle with the last-named at the northern point—lies the country which yields the best Parmesan cheese. The fields are of three kinds, those nearly always under water, those irrigated, and those used for rotation crops. The cattle that are utilised for cheese-making are mostly Swiss bred, and being valuable are well looked after. They are stalled at sundown in the buildings attached to the great farms, where farmhouse, cottages, barns and stables are all enclosed within a high wall. The little rectangular patches of meadow on which they feed are enclosed by rows of poplars or willows which make the landscape very monotonous. In winter a dense fog often shrouds the countryside and a deadly chill pervades the atmosphere, while the humidity of summer, when the sun draws the moisture from the soaking earth, is very enervating.

BERGAMO

WHEN October comes in its yearly round and the autumn afternoons close in, it is sometimes good to sit idly outside a caffè with the pernicious cigarette and ruminate on the glories of a past summer—better this than to hustle up the street a sight-seeing. A hot day was ending and the Bergamo of mediæval times towered above the haze of a sun-baked land and the smoke that curled upwards in thin wreaths from the city below. "La Città Alta" thus raised its head proudly against the copper-coloured sky, thrusting its bulwarks to the edge of one of the last spurs of the Alps that here creep down on to the plain. What a grand prospect from the shady boulevard on those ramparts which encircle the old fortress! The sun has not yet set; beneath lies the Borgo S. Leonardo, the lower city, a busy place with factory chimneys on its outskirts; beyond, a sea of verdure, cut by lines of tall poplars and here and there a slender *campanile*, stretches away over Lombardy until lost in the haze past the towers and domes of Monza, Cremona, and distant Milan.

There is something very fascinating in the quiet and exclusive old city. Its streets are steep and narrow, its houses seem to rake the sky, the rattle of wheels does not often disturb the aristocratic silence, a silence accentuated tenfold when one has left behind its busy plebeian partner on the plain below, and whisked upwards by the funicular, found oneself suddenly amidst high walls. Great spaces of faced stone are these walls, pierced by tiny windows, almost forbidding in their austerity; and though glimpses of foliage and flowering creepers break through, the pervading air is one of mystery and intrigue.

In the wars with Austria, Bergamo was a great rallying-point for patriots and a continual thorn in the side of that polyglot empire. The names of heroic Bergamasque who died for their country are inscribed on sundry tablets on the walls under the old Brotello. This interesting building stands at one end of the little Piazza Garibaldi, and is somewhat similar to the one which forms the illustration to Como, with the difference that here a fine open stairway leads up to the first floor. The great hall is now occupied as a library. In a corner at the head of the stairs rises a massive quadrangular belfry, one of the prominent features in the outline of "La Città Alta."

17

Figure 4: BERGAMO

BERGAMO

Beyond the Brotello lies the Cathedral, a well-proportioned Renaissance building, which, by its juxtaposition to the much more ancient church of Sta Maria Maggiore, looks comparatively of recent date. It is constructed entirely of white marble and has a good dome. A Madonna by G. Bellini behind the high altar is its great treasure, and the only thing in it worthy of notice.

Sta Maria is an early Lombard pile of buildings, with a very lofty tower and an octagon over the crossing, which rises in four galleried storeys surmounted by a low spire. Good galleries extend round the exterior of the apse, and side chapels are thrust out at odd places with no particular plan. The east porch is by far the most interesting feature, and is an elaborate piece of work in *breccia* and white marble. The supporting pillars rest on the backs of two lions, the old ecclesiastical symbol of strength, the columns of the portal are beautifully sculptured, and one of them, encircled with admirable figures, is very fine. Above is a canopy under which, on his horse, sits King Lupus with two attendants, while beneath a second canopy on top are statuettes of the Virgin and Child, and the two Marys. The west porch is almost similar to this, but of not so intricate a design. It has also no canopies, but is surmounted by a turret niche, let into the wall of the main building, in which is the figure of the patroness. The doors of these two portals are of superbly grained rosewood. They open into the transepts, which are the finest portions of the interior, the carved choir stalls and screen by Stefano da Bergamo are considered the best in Italy.

Adjoining the east porch is the Capella Colleoni, the mausoleum of Bartolommeo Colleoni the celebrated *condottiere* of the fifteenth century, whose equestrian statue in front of the church of SS. Giovanni e Paolo in Venice is remarkable, not only as a work of art, but as exemplifying the power and rugged strength of a great man.

The façade is terribly ornate, with chequer work in white and black marble, red and yellow busts and medallions, twisted pillars and strange arabesques. The interior contains the tomb of Bartolommeo who sits astride his horse. It is rather too elaborate to be entirely pleasing. At the south end is one of the finest examples of *intarsia*, or inlaid wood-work, in Italy. The subjects of the three panels represent the entry into Jerusalem, and scenes from the stirring times in which the great *condottiere* played so prominent a part. The backgrounds are evidently of landscape in the neighbourhood. Not only is the spirit and execution of this fine work extremely good, but the colour surpasses anything of the sort I have seen. It is kept under lock and key, enclosed in three rosewood panels of well-selected grain. Not far from the chapel is the house in which Donizetti died. The Borgo S. Leonardo is of older date than "La Città Alta," although it is the more modern of the two. On the base of a damaged Corinthian column standing in the small piazza of Sta Maria d'Oleono is an old Latin inscription which tells that the column was erected where once stood a heathen temple, and that S. Alessandro, standard-bearer to the Theban Legion, overthrew the heathen pillar by a miracle, the column being erected by members of the municipality with the alms of the faithful. It is doubtful whether the Pergamus of ancient writers is the city on the hill or its sister on the plain; this relic rather points to the latter as the site. In the Borgo a fair, held for a month from the middle of August, and known as the Fiera di Sant' Alessandro, has taken place without intermission since the tenth century—surely a record; and there is no doubt that in the ancient Italian drama, harlequin, personifying the manners and jargon of the neighbouring Val Brembana, was a Bergamasque, and originated at this ancient festival.

BRESCIA

BRESCIA, like Bergamo, is situated on the fringe of the mountains and the plains, and like Bergamo played an important part in the wars against Austria. Its *castello* stands high above the rest of the city, but in the face of the power possessed of modern arms it would not be worth a garrison. So its ramparts and entrenchments have been wisely converted into a pleasant garden from which wide views of rolling country and level plain extend.

Many traces of the Roman colony of Brescia remain, but it was due to a small boy of the virile race that populate the city that the most interesting was unearthed. When a child, Girolamo Ioli was much exercised in mind about a Corinthian column that stuck out of the ground and around which he was wont to play. In maturer years the curiosity of youth was still the ruling passion, and he made it his business to agitate. Like many another agitator his demands were in time gratified, and excavations were commenced which resulted in the unearthing of a building erected by Vespasian it is supposed in the year 72—the supposition resting on fragmentary inscriptions. Palace of Justice or temple, this building is now the museum, and contains one of the finest bronzes Italy can boast of. Found in 1826, this beautiful winged figure of Victory, which is six feet high, still bears a trace of the silver fillet interwoven with a wreath of laurel-leaves that bound her hair. The last-century additions of a shield, which she was thought to have held, and a helmet under one of her feet, have been removed, and Victory stands in the state in which she was discovered. The head and limbs are finely modelled, and the arrangement of the drapery could not be excelled.

Down the wide street in front of the Museum a Corinthian column and heavy frieze, supported by massive brick pillars, have been excavated. Opposite these relics is the huge Martinengo Palace. In a line due south is the church of Sta Afra built on the site of a temple to Saturn. Most of the houses in the vicinity have Roman masonry in their basements and Roman inscriptions let into their walls. From this one gathers that ancient Brixia occupied this part of the later city. Write it down to the credit of Brescia that her citizens passed a law as early as 1480 that all antiquities found should be preserved and given up to the town.

There are two cathedrals in Brescia, La Rotunda and the Duomo Nuovo.

The former is one of the most interesting ecclesiastical buildings in Italy. Constructed of stone, with a red brick dog-tooth cornice and twenty-four brick arches, supported by white marble pilasters forming an arcade into which the exterior is divided, a most pleasing effect is obtained. In the interior a circular colonnade, composed of eight extremely massive four-sided piers bearing round arches, supports the stone dome. It is supposed to be of seventh-century construction, and is evidently on the site of an earlier Roman building, as fragments of a mosaic floor exist beneath the present one. This, which is partly tesselated, is much below the level of the ground outside. Lower still, beneath the presbytery and choir, down twenty steps, is a very ancient crypt, in which forty marble columns support the round arches that carry the weight of the fabric above. None of these columns is more than five feet high. Half a dozen blocked up lights, with bases not more than three feet from the floor, are evidence that outside, the level of the ground was at one time far below where it is at present.

The Duomo Nuovo is a finely proportioned edifice and one of the best seventeenth-century churches in the country. The façade is immense and gains by its simplicity. The fine dome is said to be the third in size in Italy; and the lofty interior of white marble, unspoilt by any colour or decoration, gains in space from the fact that there is but one bay to the nave, producing the effect on the senses that one is everywhere standing under the spacious height of Brescia's greatest landmark. The houses of the piazza outside are chiefly occupied by metal-workers, and those who know the incessant din produced by the tapping of their hammers, will quite understand that it was impossible to make a sketch of these two churches as they stand together.

Figure 5: BRESCIA

Adjoining the Duomo Nuovo is the Brotello with its fine Torre del Popolo, an embattled tower. The inner courtyard is partly of red brick with a good corridor of the thirteenth century, formed of pointed and round arches and brick groining. Another fine tower stands in the Piazza Vecchia, the Torre del' Orologio. Its enormous dial marks the hours from I to XXIV, the course of the sun and moon, and has the signs of the Zodiac displayed on its face. Two figures that stand on top of the tower strike the hours in a similar way to those on the Clock Tower of Venice. At the west end of the piazza is La Loggia, the town hall, a good example of an early sixteenth-century building. It was commenced, to be accurate, by Tornasso Formentone in 1492 and continued from his designs as far as the first floor. Sansovino was responsible for the second, and Palladio completed what the other two had begun. The building, however, as a whole, is superb. Magnificent arches support the first floor, to which a grand open staircase leads. The medallions and figures which adorn the exterior are extremely good, and the frieze and cornice are equally so. The rich colour of the marble employed lends a beautiful tone to a beautiful building. Unfortunately the interior was burnt out in January 1575. The fire which consumed it is supposed to have originated at the instigation of those who wished to destroy certain ancient charters granting liberties to the inhabitants.

The Torre della Pallata is in a corner of the square—a good specimen of castellated architecture, which rises from a sloping base of immense stones and terminates with a projecting turret.

Brescia contains many fine palaces, and from the streets into which they open one often gets a glimpse, through the iron grille of their portals, of a charming arcaded court. The splash of a flower embowered fountain is music to ear and the cool shade under the arches a rest for eye.

VERONA

THOSE who enter the Brenner Pass, and with faces set towards Italy, leave Innsbruck behind, may have noticed how, after toilsome puffing and straining uphill, the train suddenly seems to draw breath and glide smoothly onwards with increased pace. At the side of the iron road a little thread of water dances merrily over a pebble bed in its haste to reach the sunny plains that lie to the south of the great mountain barrier. Further on the rail and its sparkling attendant part company to join later, when, from their slender origin, the waters have become a rushing river—the river Adige. The mountains are behind, to the north; the character of the landscape has changed, and within a horseshoe bend of the swift stream, well-nigh enclosed by it, lies Verona.

Verona "La Degna," Verona the Worthy, a city crammed with the history of past wars, a city of colour, in its bricks, in its stones, in its marble walls and fresco adorned palaces. Wherever one turns, be it the pale green of the river on which the wheels of those watermills, so like the Noah's Ark of childhood's days, for ever turn, or the brilliant and keen blue of the sky, there is always colour for the eye in Verona. Colour for the mind too lies concealed in its streets and buildings. Greek, Roman, Ostrogoth and Frank, Italians and Austrians, have all ruled here. Ruled and gone and left their trace on this beautiful city—the key to Alt' Italia—which Italy once more holds and guards with jealous eye. Long may she keep it.

Verona is connected with two great names in the history of Italian architecture, Frà Giaconda, the monk who in the early days of Renaissance was supreme in the north, and Sanmicheli. Many of the fine palaces the former designed bear evidence of his talent and justify the summons to Rome, where he went at an advanced age to superintend the building of St. Peter's. The latter, who evolved the triangular and pentangular bastion, is more widely known in the science of fortification than as a builder. Frà Giacondo's finest work in Verona is undoubtedly the Palazzo del Consiglio, the old town hall called "La Loggia," which stands on the north side of the Piazza dei Signori, one of the most architecturally beautiful squares in Italy. The Palazzo della Ragione, with a courtyard and grand open stairway of the fourteenth century, is on the south of the square next door to the Tribunale, and the Prefettura is opposite. The fine portal of the latter is one of Sanmicheli's works. These magnificent buildings, with the exception of the first-named, were all at one time or another palaces of the great family of Scaligeri or Della Scala, and in one of them Dante, whose statue is in the centre of the Piazza, found refuge when driven from Florence.

The family of Scaligeri, although settled in Verona as early as 1085, comes first before the historian at the death of the bloody tyrant Ezzelino in 1261. Verona, freed from his terrible rule, became at that date a free town, and Mastino della Scala accepted the office of Capitano del Popolo. Onwards for over a hundred years the Scaligeri governed Verona; and during the reign of the most famous of the race, Francesco, or "Can Grande," Great Dog, it became the gathering-place for men of note of all sorts, and his palace the home of the great poet. The family crest, a ladder, is to be seen all over the city, while the unique group of the Scala tombs is without a parallel.

This wonderful group stands outside the little church of Sta Maria Antica at the end of a passage leading out of the Piazza dei Signori.

Of these tombs, that of Mastino I. is a simple sarcophagus ornamented with nothing but a cross. It was at one time covered with a canopy, but the stones of this, being handy, were used for the restoration of Sta Maria Antica close by. The tomb of Can Grande forms the canopy over the portal of this church. Columns support its three storeys. Upon a sarcophagus lies an effigy of the Great Dog with his good sword at his side; above is his equestrian statue in full armour. Mastino II, who succeeded his uncle Can Grande, is likewise represented by a recumbent figure on the sarcophagus of his tomb, which is also crowned by an equestrian statue in armour. The visor of his helmet is drawn down, and thereby hangs the tale that Mastino was ashamed to show his face, even to his wife, after he had treacherously slain with his own sword his relative, Bishop Bartolommeo della Scala. Can Signorio's monument, though not the most elaborate, is decidedly the finest. At the four corners under beautiful pointed canopies, are the figures of Sigismundo, Alexius, St. George, and Signorio himself. A great deal of the bronze work and detail about this tomb is very good, and the equestrian figure on the top is excellent. There, gathered together, these warrior princes of the great family repose in their last long sleep. Those who deem the pen mightier than the sword, may care to reflect that a fame more universal and lasting than that of all the Delia Scalas has been attained by a French scholar of the sixteenth century who also bore the name of Scaliger. Yet even this prince of learning was prouder of his traditional descent from the noble Veronese house than of all his achievements in the world of letters.

Figure 6: THE PORCH OF THE CATHEDRAL, VERONA

THE PORCH OF THE CATHEDRAL, VERONA

And Verona's churches? Tradition says that Charlemagne erected the first building on the site of the Cathedral. The present edifice, though almost entirely reconstructed in the fifteenth century, was commenced in the tenth. The most ancient part that remains, probably a portion of the first church, is the apse, which on its exterior bears traces of Roman influence. It is very simply built of a small cut grey freestone, faced with flat pilasters terminating in Roman capitals, above which is a frieze of floral pattern. In the remainder of the building Verona marble and the rich yellow stone of the district are used.

The double-arched west porch of the twelfth century is exceptionally good. Two colossal gryphons support elegant columns, and still command a certain amount of awe amongst the smaller children who play about the Piazza del Duomo. Both arches are round; the lower is supported by four columns, the upper by eight. Representations on the inner shafts of the lower arch of the two Paladins, Roland and Oliver, give a semblance to the tradition that

Charlemagne had something to do with the first church erected here. Oliver holds his celebrated sword, on which is inscribed *Du-rin-dar-da*. Roland is cross-legged and bears his shield. They are both seen in the illustration. The colour of this porch and façade is very beautiful. Great blocks of red marble intermingle with yellow stone, white and pink marble courses continue the construction above, and arabesques of a weathered grey stone complete the harmony. The fine south portal is an earlier erection. Some ancient frescoes decorate the lunette, and monsters grin at one like a nightmare from above.

The interior is lofty and very striking. Tremendous columns support the low Gothic roof, the vaulting of which hardly exceeds the height of the arches between the nave and aisles. Many signs of "giving way" and cracks in the masonry have necessitated iron girders, which detract somewhat from a fine effect. The heavy capitals of the nave columns are rendered rather unsightly by three courses of floral design. The aisles are pointed, narrow, and very good. Encircling the high altar is a colonnade screen, which though beautiful in itself and designed by Sanmicheli, is sadly out of place. The fine bronze crucifix which surmounts it is by Gianbattista da Verona.

The cloisters lie on the north side of the Cathedral. About half a dozen feet below the level of the pavement, standing on its base, is a fine Corinthian column, with a Roman floor around. Between them and the early Lombard church of S. Giovanni in Fonte is a tortuous corridor lined with sepulchral slabs of many archbishops and bishops. This little dark church is formed of four small bays and was formerly the old baptistery. In the centre of the nave stands a huge octagonal font, with a smaller one inside, wherein stood the officiating priest. The figures in bas-relief on these two fonts, which by the way are cut from one solid block of marble, are well worth studying.

Another Gothic church is Sant' Anastasia, which was commenced by the Dominicans in the thirteenth century and is still incomplete. The nave is very fine and has the same low vaulting that is a feature in the Cathedral; its walls, too, are cracked and held together by iron girders. Close to the west door in the interior are two humpbacked figures which hold the Holy Water basins and are of some interest. One of them was executed by the father of Paolo Veronese and the other by Alessandro Rossi, who took his cripple son "Gobbino" for his model.

The most interesting ecclesiastical fabric in the city is, however, the church of San Zenone. It is unspoilt by anything flamboyant or gaudy, and is a fine example of Romanesque architecture—some consider it the finest in North Italy. A ninth-century building stood here before the present structure was begun in 1138. The west façade is marble, the apse and sides of alternating brick and marble courses. The great portal is a most elaborate example of early twelfth-century work, on which are rudely sculptured knights engaging in deadly combat, scriptural subjects and imitations of Roman bas-reliefs with Latin inscriptions. Theodoric on horseback, with feet in stirrups—a very early representation of such—and Roman dress, engages in the chase of the deer with the Devil. The attendant dogs are evil spirits furnished to the Emperor by the Arch-fiend. The ninth-century bronze doors are very remarkable and consist of forty-two square plates fixed on to pine-wood. The subjects of each panel, which are Biblical, are most interesting; some of the little figures wear the conical flat-brimmed hat that may still be seen on the heads of the shepherds in the more remote districts of Venetia. These doors boast no handles, but two huge grotesque heads do duty instead, and are the means of opening and closing them. Above the portal is a wheel-of-fortune window executed by Briolotus. At the top is the figure of a king, and at the bottom lies a prostrate man; between these two are many figures climbing up and falling down in their efforts to reach the best place. The façade terminates in a gable, with a lean-to on either side.

Figure 7: INTERIOR OF S. ZENO, VERONA

INTERIOR OF S. ZENO, VERONA

The interior is very striking, not only in its good proportions but in its simplicity, which no side-altars mar. As in the cathedral at Chester, one enters from the west down a flight of steps, held a moment in admiration by the solemn grandeur of this fine church. The beautiful larch roof soars away far above the mellowed floor, the warm colour of the walls and depth of shadow through the arches of the crypt below the choir, create a harmony of colour from our point of vantage not often met with in Italy's churches. The aisles are divided from the nave by alternate piers and red marble pillars, the former with ascending Doric pilasters, two of which, near the west end, support a flying arch beneath the roof and are evident traces of an early vaulting. At the end of the nave, and occupying its last three bays, is the raised choir reached by two flights of marble steps on either side of those leading down into the crypt. On the red marble balustrade of the choir are figures of Christ and the twelve apostles. In a niche on the south side is a forbidding looking figure of S. Zeno, the patron saint of the city, who, being an African, is represented with a black face. The apse at the east end was rebuilt in the fifteenth century and has Gothic windows.

The old Benedictine cloisters of the once attached monastery stand on the north, and contain amongst other tombs twenty-nine of the Della Scalas. The cloisters and tombs are admirably preserved. The former consists of brick arches, pointed on the east and west, and round on the north and south, supported by coupled columns of red marble. Of Verona's forty churches these three are the most typical and interesting, and San Zenone, with its great architectural simplicity and wonderful *campanile*, holds the palm.

It is a city of shapely bell-towers; every church has one. Some are high, others low and unpretending; some are flat topped, others embattled or crowned by the red brick spire which greets one further west in the lake country. But the most beautiful of all is that which stands at a corner of the Piazza dei Signori, adjoining the Palazzo della Ragione, and rears its head over two hundred and fifty feet from the pavement below. Like a queen, this graceful Campanile del Municipio stands, dominating her subjects the other towers, with all the tinkling bells they contain. Across the river from the vantage-ground of the terrace on the hill beneath the Castello S. Pietro, Verona lies mapped out. Her dull red and brown roofs remind one of the harmonious colours of a Bokharan rug. Immediately below, at the foot of the hill, are the ruins of the Roman theatre, and the green waters of the Adige, rushing under the arches of the old stone bridge close by. Straight as a line ran the Roman street to the Porta dei Borsari, erected under the Emperor Gallienus in 265, and out into the country beyond. Between this old gateway, which stands athwart the street almost blocking it, and the river, is mediæval Verona, intersected and crossed by hundreds of *vicoli*, or lanes, and full of subjects for a painter's brush in the *cortili* that fringe them. At the corner of the Vicola Pigna and the "Alley of the Jutting Stone," is a low marble column with a huge fir-cone on the top, a reminiscence of Roman days. Near at hand is the fine palace that Sanmicheli erected for the Miniscalchi family, and in a lane a few steps away, a crumbling remnant of another fine house with a beautiful portal and row of windows. These are but a few things in the secluded byways of old Verona, where one's feet continually led one on journeys of discovery. Many a silent and deserted courtyard I found, where the grass shyly thrust its head between the cobblestones, and where creepers came wantonly trailing down over old walls in a sweet endeavour to hide the decay of man's handiwork.

From all these it is but a step to the focus of the city's life, the Piazza delle Erbe, the forum of Roman rule, and the most picturesque market square in Italy. In the centre—and seen in the sketch—is the small open tribune which occupies the place of an old building where the newly elected Capitano del Popolo was invested with the insignia of his office. The fountain farther up the square was erected by Berengarius in 916, and supplied with fresh water by Can Signorio. The figure surmounting it gazes stonily every day over a sea of umbrellas which shelter the market folk below. Can Signorio beautified his native city, and erected the tower at the end of the piazza—a tower which can boast of the first public clock. The Lion of St. Mark stands on an isolated column, surrounded by vegetable and fruit stalls, in front of the Palazzo Tresa, a highly ornate specimen of the seventeenth century. Many of the old houses still bear traces of the frescoes which covered them, and which at one time must have made Verona's streets veritable galleries of decorative art. Others retain the marble balconies which formed so fascinating a feature of the city's architecture.

Figure 8: THE MARKET PLACE, VERONA

THE MARKET PLACE, VERONA

Of earlier days there still remains one of the grandest ruins in Italy—the celebrated Amphitheatre. It was the night of a hot day; a blood-red moon, mounting on her upward path in the copper-coloured sky, left a grim mass of deep shadow beneath. Bats were hawking in and out of the black shadow, as yet unrelieved by the electric lights, and the spacious piazza was nearly empty. An ominous feeling, intensified by the distant hum of the busier parts of the city, unsettled one's nerves. My thoughts travelled back to the time when, there behind that gloomy mass, slaves would be cleansing the arena after a scene of cruel sport, and the distant hum was nothing but the excited throngs discussing the brutal slaughter. Did the great poet in his twilight wanderings ever see such a moon and such a sky? It was certainly an evening that would have enticed him to shun the noisy company of his fellow men and saunter alone in the shadow of the great Amphitheatre. Perhaps his spirit was there now. Small wonder that in my dreams that night the howls of a cruel audience and the gentleness of the lonely poet were mixed up in inextricable confusion.

PADUA

The quaint old city of Padua lies on the beaten track to Venice. In its great Basilica repose the remains of St. Anthony. Giotto's frescoes in the Church of the Madonna are still a glory to behold, its university is one of the oldest in Europe, and the modern epicure can drink coffee of the very best at Pedrocchi's, an establishment as well known amongst Italians as the celebrated Florian's at Venice. The origin of Padua goes back to Antenor, whose tomb occupies a corner near the Ponte de Lorenzo close to the house at one time inhabited by Dante. A sarcophagus was discovered in 1274 during excavations for the building of a foundling hospital, and when opened, a skeleton of immense size, one hand still gripping a sword, was seen inside. Who could it be but Antenor? There was Virgil's authority for it that he had founded Padua—so Antenor it was who lay there in his stone coffin, and the good folk of Padua carried the sarcophagus and its contents to the church of S. Lorenzo amidst great excitement. The church has been demolished but the tomb was spared.

Padua's tortuous streets are lined with arcades, and although modern requirements have ordained that some should be altered and the houses pulled down, it still preserves an air of mediæval antiquity. Situated on the winding little river Bacchiglione and intersected by other small streams, it forms in the itinerary of the tourist a sort of prelude to Venice. Innumerable bridges span these waterways. Some of them are of Roman construction; and wherever one's footsteps lead one, be it along the *riviere*—the open streets that run by the side of the streams—or the narrow ways that may be likened to a rabbit warren, the great charm of bygone days lingers in them all, and still clings to its old walls and bridges.

The Cathedral, with an incomplete façade, was not finished till 1754. It is a vast, ugly structure of brick with a *campanile* and dome. The whitewashed interior possesses no redeeming feature; unless it be a rather pleasing course of grey marble that runs round on a level with the capitals of the grey columns. A bust of Petrarch, who was a canon here, and some beautiful twelfth-century MSS. with exquisite miniatures in the sacristy, are the most interesting things it contains. If there is but little in the Cathedral worthy of notice there is much in the other churches of Padua.

Figure 9: THE CATHEDRAL, PADUA

THE CATHEDRAL, PADUA

Sta Giustiana is a very fine building of the sixteenth century, commenced from designs by Padre Girolamo da Brescia and finished fifty years later by Andrea Morone. All its altars are decorated with scrolls and floral patterns, in the inlaid marble work for which Italy has been famous for many generations.

The church of S. Agostino degli Eremitani is a solemn building of a single nave three hundred feet in length, which was constructed at the latter end of the thirteenth century. Its sacristy is used by the students of the university as their chapel, and many memorials of the most famous among them cover its walls. The tombs the church contains are very interesting. One with a magnificent canopy is of the fifth Lord of Padua, Jacopo di Carrara, a friend of Petrarch's, while other members of this extinct family lie buried in the church. The Carraras were Lords of Padua for many generations; the last of the great race with his two sons held the city in 1405 against the Venetians, but famine so reduced the garrison that they surrendered themselves to the besiegers and were conveyed prisoners to Venice. The Council of Ten decreed that they should be strangled in their cells, and a member of the noble Venetian family of Priuli performed this disgraceful murder in the dungeons of the Doge's palace.

Sta Maria dell' Arena, or the church of the Madonna of the Arena, stands practically in what was the Roman Amphitheatre. About the year 1306, a certain Enrico Scrovengo, who was owner of the Arena and adjacent land, built within its precincts a chapel of the Annunciation, known as Sta Maria dell' Arena. Giotto was working in Padua at the time, and Enrico recognising his talent employed him to build and decorate the little chapel. It consists of a single nave with a Gothic apse, and tiny sacristy in which is a monument to the founder, whose tomb is behind the altar. It is not the province of this book to deal with the pictorial art of the country, but Giotto's frescoes which cover the walls of this little church stand far above all else—not excepting Fra Angelico's beautiful decorations in the monastic cells of S. Marco at Florence—in the deep piety and tender expression of intense religious feeling they portray.

The greatest church that Padua possesses is the huge building dedicated to S. Antonio—"il Santo," as he is called by the Padovanese. This enormous fabric of marble and brick, stands facing a wide open piazza on two sides of which are low houses—houses of three storeys are very rare in the older parts of the city. Opposite the façade is Donatello's grand equestrian statue of Erasmo da Narni, or Gattamelata, bearing his name, "Opus Donatelli Flor." In the piazza is the Scuoio del Santo and the little church of San Giorgio, the sepulchral chapel of the Sograna family; close by which is the tomb of Rolando Piazzola with a fine Gothic canopy.

The seven domes of S. Antonio cluster round a heavy central spire, and two beautiful bell-towers rise elegantly to a height above; from wherever one sees the church, these domes and spires compose and "pile" well. Il Santo died in 1231, and Padua decided to erect a suitable building to hold his sacred remains. Niccolò Pisano was requisitioned for the task, but was not given a free hand. He was informed that he must follow the fashion of the day and produce a real Gothic edifice. His failure to carry out these instructions can be best seen in the façade, where the three portals are very poor; nevertheless, and despite his leanings towards other styles, he was able to introduce something of the Gothic in his bell-towers, in the open galleries round the exterior of the apse, and the arcading of the west front, with a mixed result that has produced a really stupendous church. The best decoration of the exterior is contained in the three west doors of bronze, which are exceedingly good.

The fine interior is most impressive, but what the result will be when the present scheme of decoration, already begun in the choir and apse, is carried out, it is difficult to say. The chapel of Il Santo is half way up the north aisle. Lights burn day and night before the altar, beneath which repose the saint's remains. Four fine columns support the somewhat heavy frieze of the great Renaissance screen by Sansovino, which separates it from the aisle. Two of these columns have a charming idea in their capitals, where little sea-horses take the place of the acanthus leaf. The screen is terminated by two very beautiful pilasters adorned with exquisite arabesques. The interior of this interesting chapel is lined with nine reliefs, one of which, by Sansovino, is rather curious and certainly very gruesome. The sculptor has represented a suicide with a gaping crowd of women surrounding him in his self-inflicted death agonies. Two enormous silver candlesticks, partly of Gothic and partly Renaissance design, stand at the foot of the steps of the altar, and bronze figures and silver angels are placed upon the balustrade. In the vestibule between this chapel and the next hang hundreds of votive offerings of all descriptions, forming a museum of the tangible homage paid to the saint by his devotees. The next chapel is the only part left of an ancient fabric which stood here long before the good Padovanese raised the present magnificent church as a memorial of their venerated saint.

In the south aisle, opposite to and corresponding with Il Santo's chapel, is one dedicated to S. Felix, which is fronted by a good screen decorated with an effective fish-scale pattern of Verona marble. It contains a good altar, placed high above a flight of steps, and some interesting fourteenth-century frescoes. A thick coating of paint quite spoils the well-carved Gothic stalls, and it is to be hoped that when the scheme of decoration reaches this chapel these fine stalls will be scraped and then left in their pristine state. In another chapel are the tombs of Gattamelata and his son; these and two monuments designed by Sanmicheli on two of the piers of the nave are the best in the church.

The presbytery is cut off from the nave by a low balustrade, in the centre of which, rising in a bold sweep, is a very fine bronze gate. The High Altar, impressively placed at the top of some steps, has eight splendid panels containing bas-reliefs by Donatello. The master was also responsible for the fine group of the Madonna and Saints, as well as the huge crucifix, which are placed above it. The magnificent bronze candelabrum, which stands to the left of the altar, is twelve feet high. Its maker, Andrea Riccio, spent ten years over the work before he considered it fit to leave his studio. The figures at the base are symbolical of Music, History, Destiny, and Astrology, forming with those above, a paschal candlestick that is one of the finest pieces of bronze work in any church in the country. The sanctuary beyond the apse was an addition of the year 1693, and occupies the most eastern dome seen in the illustration. Great gilded sliding doors hide a wonderful example of fifteenth-century goldsmith's work, a casket with Il Santo's tongue inside, and many other sacred relics, as well as Gattamelata's marshal's baton. The great doors are surrounded by work of the late seventeenth century, an example of the bad taste and very low ebb ecclesiastical art had sunk to at that period. Cherubs and nude female figures playing stringed instruments—angels apparently—circle round S. Antonio, who is borne aloft by other nudes. The extravagance of the whole thing is a jarring note amongst much that is extremely fine.

The monks of the brotherhood of S. Antonio still inhabit the conventual

buildings attached to the church, and their dark-robed figures pass silently
to and fro in the cloistered courts of the monastery. The walls of these three
courts are lined with fine tombs and memorial slabs, and it was from one
of these cloisters the illustration was taken. A great magnolia tree grows on
the well-kept grass which covers the ground like green velvet. No sound from
the outside world penetrated this sequestered nook. The only note to break
the silence was the drowsy hum from a voice at prayer in one of the little
green-shuttered rooms above, and the occasional twittering of a canary in its
cage. One worked undisturbed at those domes and towers which compose so
well and seem to reach up to the very heavens.

Figure 10: S. ANTONIO, PADUA

S. ANTONIO, PADUA

Padua's university was founded in 1221 by the Emperor Frederick II. on
the site of the Inn of the Ox, and is still called il Bò. Its handsome courtyard,
attributed to Palladio, is adorned with armorial bearings of distinguished
alumni. At the head of the great staircase is a statue to Elena Piscopia, a

poetess, musician, and fluent linguist; she received a doctor's degree and died a spinster in 1684. The anatomical theatre is the oldest in Europe. Among other famous men connected with il Bò the names of Baldus, who taught law, and Galileo, who expounded mathematics, must be mentioned.

Padua also possesses the oldest Botanical Gardens in Europe, which were instituted by the Venetian Senate in 1543. Many of the exotics which grow now all over Europe were first established here, brought from the East by Venetian traders, and the botanist can spend many interesting hours in this well cared for and shady retreat.

A vast building with a remarkable history occupies one whole side of the market square. A much-travelled architect and engineer, Fra Giovanni, visited Padua in the fourteenth century, bringing with him drawings of an Indian palace; these so pleased the Padovanese that he was asked to construct a roof to their great hall, the three divisions of which had been destroyed by fire. Fra Giovanni set to work, and his vaulted wooden ceiling, one of the largest in Europe, stands covering the principal chamber of the Palazzo della Ragione, though the roof above was renewed in 1857. The paintings on the walls of this magnificent room have by degrees replaced a series of frescoes by Giotto. They are mostly mystical and symbolical, the best among them being those representing Justice and Prudence. The wooden horse which stands in the hall is supposed to have been the model for Donatello's bronze horse on which Gattamelata is seated in the famous equestrian statue outside S. Antonio. The fine *loggia* on the ground floor of the palazzo is of later date than the original parts of the building, which were designed by Pietro Cozzo and constructed in the years 1172 to 1219. In a street not far off is another beautiful building, the early-Renaissance Loggia del Consiglio, with its fine stairway and open arcade. In front of this is an antique column with the Lion of S. Mark, the sign that the city at one time belonged to the Republic of Venice. Many other houses in this quaint old town are of great interest, and the windings of its streams as they meander past rose-covered walls and low roofs, with perhaps a tapering *campanile* or a dome towering above, afford a rare field for endeavours with the pencil and brush.

VENICE

VENICE, which has no counterpart in the world, is a city of all others in which one can linger on in a dream taking no count of time. The days run into weeks, these spread themselves into months, and it becomes more and more difficult to tear oneself away from the entrancing "Mistress of the Seas," from her Cathedral and all her other marvellous buildings; from her seductive gondolas and silent canals; from her picture galleries, and alas! from the fragrant coffee we sip idling away the time under the colonnade outside Florian's in the Piazza.

Well, the seductive cup is drained and while our cigarette is alight let us look round. Directly opposite to us, on the north side of this grand square, stretches the long colonnade of the Procuratie Vecchie, built early in the sixteenth century as a habitation for the procurators of S. Mark. It is one of the best examples of early Renaissance architecture in Italy; nobler, simpler than the Procuratie Nuove where we sit, which was built in the last quarter of the same century. An arcaded building in the classical style erected by Napoleon in 1810 connects the western extremities of the two Procuratie. It is a pity that this great Renaissance Piazza should be completed by an inferior bit of modern work instead of such a brilliant gem of the Renaissance style as Sansovino's Libreria Vecchia—at present invisible to us round the corner. To this building, which faces the Doge's Palace, no higher tribute could be given than to say that its perfection fairly distracts the admiration of the onlooker from the wonderful Gothic pile before it.

But all this is *Hamlet* without the Prince. It is time to leave the shadow of the arches, to step out into the open, and to surrender ourselves to the spell of the great church which draws one with an irresistible fascination from the first moment we set foot in the Piazza. S. Mark's rises bounding the vision at the eastern end of the great square with its gorgeous façade and cool grey domes. So rich is the colouring and so strange the outline that one wonders almost whether architecture has not passed here into the sister art of painting.

Figure 11: S. MARK'S, VENICE

S. MARK'S, VENICE

Yes, there stands a building surpassingly fascinating, unique and outside all comparison with any other church in the country. Planned as a Greek Cross, like S. Sophia at Constantinople, it is reminiscent of the East far more than any building in the peninsula, or even in Sicily where some with direct Arab influence still exist. The great traders of Venice who lavished their wealth on its decoration, and whose every homeward bound ship brought back from the Orient a choice column, a rare piece of marble, or some such thing as a contribution towards its making, helped to raise it bit by bit until the wonderful church grew to be what we find it to-day, the most seductive ecclesiastical fabric in Italy.

It was not until the year 1807 that S. Mark's became the Cathedral church of Venice. Before this date the Patriarchal seat was the church of S. Pietro di Castello, and S. Mark's simply the chapel attached to the Doge's Palace. In 828 the body of the Evangelist, stolen from Alexandria, was brought to Venice and S. Theodore the tutelary saint deposed to make way for a more important patron. S. Mark's remains were then placed in a church which was destroyed by fire in 976. The following year saw the first stone laid of a building which is perhaps the most interesting in Christendom; but it was not until eighty years had passed that the walls were finished, and seventy more gone by before it was consecrated. The interior sustaining walls are brick, and are lined with marble or covered with mosaics and decorated with every sort of inlay. The *tout ensemble* of this is an extraordinarily harmonious mixture of styles which compels unceasing admiration.

Standing at the west end of the Piazza one sees, almost stretching across the further side, a marvellous façade of deep shadowed arches; the tympanums seem to sparkle with jewels; the arches are supported by what appears to be a forest of columns, orderly in rank, receding into the shadow. Above, to give quality to this shade, is a flat surface that runs from end to end of the façade, broken by a central semicircular window, and crowned with Gothic turrets, crocketed finials and angels with wings outspread. Then, surmounting all are five wondrous domes, Oriental in themselves, so overpoweringly Oriental that the eye, unable at this distance to discriminate, telegraphs to the brain the magic words—"The East!" Spoils from the East, from Greece, from Syria, from Egypt; mosaics of the sixteenth and seventeenth centuries, bronze horses of Roman origin, Gothic saints under canopied turrets, flag poles with the crimson banner and golden Lion of S. Mark, all arranged without disorder, but all succumbing to the majesty of the marvellous domes. More Eastern than European is the Venetian's love of colour, and this is the note most deeply impressed on the mind with regard to S. Mark's—five grey domes, a foil to the brilliant mosaics and many-hued marble columns and walls below, but blending with them so subtly that the whole is one gorgeous chromatic scale.

The effect of the blazing sun pouring down on the façade at midday, casting deep shadows under the arches, is very fine. Again, in the evening when the domes are alight with the last rays of the dying orb and the great Piazza is in cool shade, the glories of the wonderful fabric assume a dramatic effect which becomes almost tragic as the light disappears and everything subsides into a monotone. Colour begets more subtlety in grey weather; every note that might jar on the eye is then diffused among the quieter tones around, and for this reason the pearly sky of a grey day was chosen to depict S. Mark's. The great *campanile* which fell to the ground on July 14, 1902, is now in course of re-erection. For some years past the necessary but hideous hoarding at its base has interfered with the beauty of the Piazza. The illustration does not show this but depicts the length of the façade, with the beautiful Porta della Carta and corner of the Doge's Palace beyond.

The lowest portion of the façade is formed as a vestibule with seven arches, the last one of which at each end is open through. All the columns and their capitals (spoils from the East) are of much older date than the building. Very few of these capitals fit the *abacus* on which they rest; most of them are exquisitely carved with foliage free from all imagery. The central arch is larger than the others. Under it is a grand door of forty-eight bronze panels inlaid with silver. The workmanship of the other doors which flank this is also very fine. The intricate Byzantine carving above these forms a scheme of decoration wherein figures, birds, beasts and arabesques run in a perfect riot of fanciful design. The vaulting of the vestibule is covered with mosaics of different periods. Those of the twelfth century are concerned with the Creation of the Firmament and the Creation of Life; the story of Adam and Eve continued on to the Deluge and Noah; the tragedy of Cain and Abel; Joseph's dream, Pharaoh and the story of Moses. The general scheme throughout is of white figures, mostly nude, on a green ground. Although not in any way comparable to the earlier mosaics at Ravenna, these are far better in style and true feeling for the enrichment of a flat surface than those of later date in the lunettes above the façade arches. Here the *raison d'être* of mosaic has been made subservient to an attempt to imitate the shades and gradations of an oil painting. The most important of these later mosaics is that which was executed from a design by Titian by the brothers Zuccati in the sixteenth century, wherein S. Mark appears in pontifical robes. It is above the centre door. On the pavement beneath is a red and white lozenge of marble marking the spot where Pope Alexander III. and Barbarossa were reconciled in July 1177, through the intervention of the Venetian Republic. Many inscribed slabs of marble bearing legends in Greek and Syriac, and Roman bas-reliefs, are let into the walls of the vestibule, evidence of offerings towards the building of the fabric. All the archivolts of the five large arches are decorated with symbolic carvings; the most interesting being that of the main entrance, where a charmingly quaint story illustrative of peasant life in the twelve months of the year tells in a realistic way the labours of those who till the soil. February with a little figure sitting at a fire warming his hands is particularly naïve.

On the south, S. Mark's joins the Doge's Palace by means of the Porta della Carta. At the base of a column which stands in an angle of the wall are four porphyry figures of knights in chain mail with arms round one another's necks. This group is supposed to have come from Acre. Detached from the main building, and not far from its south-west corner, are two short rectangular columns with Greek inscriptions. They were brought from the church of S. Saba at Ptolemais in 1256. Amongst other interesting spoils there is a slab let into the north wall on which Ceres, holding a torch in each hand, appears drawn in a chariot by two dragons. It seems to be a very early Persian work. But the best known, and certainly the finest gift the exterior of the building can boast, is that of the four bronze horses which stand over the principal entrance. Sent from Constantinople in 1204 by order of the Doge Dandolo as part of the spoils of victory when that city fell to the arms of the Venetians in the fourth Crusade, these horses at one time adorned the triumphal arch of Nero in Rome. Both Domitian and Trajan transferred them in turn to arches of their own; and Constantine conveyed them across the seas to his new capital in the East, where he also put them up over an arch. In 1797, when the Republic of Venice was no more, Napoleon took these already much-travelled horses from S. Mark's façade to Paris and placed them on the top of the Arc du Carrousel. After the peace in 1815 the Austrian Emperor, Francis I. caused them to be returned to their former position, and there they remain to-day.

Three doors open into the cathedral from the vestibule, and two on the north side. The interior strikes one at first as being very dark; but when the eye becomes accustomed to the half-light and is familiar with everything within, this wears off, and the senses are rather soothed than otherwise by the mystic gloom. Indeed, it is a great relief to find oneself inside out of the glare of the Piazza, and, seated in a corner perhaps, quietly contemplating the grand mosaics which cover the vaulting from end to end. It is quite impossible to describe these adequately in a short chapter which deals with other things as well, but noting them in guide-book fashion one observes that those in the aisles on either side of the main entrance depict the Acts and Miracles of the Apostles. On the vaulting of the dome which forms, so to speak, the foot of the Greek cross, is the Descent of the Holy Ghost. The great central dome is covered by twelfth-century mosaics of the Ascension, and the vault between this and the first dome with Christ's Passion and Resurrection. The vaulting of the two domes which compose the arms of the cross is decorated by work of later date; that on the north with the history of S. John, and that on the south with the saints. The chapel of S. John which is in the north transept was converted in the seventeenth century into one dedicated to the Miraculous Virgin of Constantinople. In the south transept also a rededication has taken place; the chapel of S. Leonard being turned into that of the Holy Sacrament.

Behind the gorgeous marble screen which divides the presbytery from the body of the church the high altar rises beneath a canopy of *verdeantico* borne by four columns. Two of these columns are eleventh century and are elaborately carved in courses of innumerable figures. They came from Pola when Venice subdued Istria, and are much more interesting than the other two of a later date; the remains of S. Mark rest within this magnificent shrine. On the screen itself stand the Evangelist, the twelve Apostles, and Mary.

At the back of the high altar is the Pala d'Oro, the greatest treasure the cathedral possesses, and the most celebrated golden altarpiece in existence. The upper part came from Constantinople in 976, the lower about the middle of the fourteenth century. It is composed of eighty-three panels of Greek and Byzantine design filled with enamelled figures, studded with uncut gems and precious stones, and covered with Greek and Latin inscriptions. More gorgeous than that of S. Ambrogio in Milan, this magnificent piece of goldsmith's art glitters and sparkles in a wonderful manner when lit up by the candles used at high mass, and is without doubt the most splendid ecclesiastical treasure in Italy.

Figure 12: INTERIOR, S. MARK'S, VENICE

INTERIOR, S. MARK'S, VENICE

The fifth or eastern dome which is over the presbytery is covered with mosaics representing Christ and the Prophets, and one that is hardly visible of S. Mark is on the walls of the east end. The great figure of Christ faces the church and in its simplicity is very impressive.

The gallery, which is where the triforium would be in a Gothic building, runs round the whole cathedral and is pierced on its inner side only. The walls at the back and above are decorated with more mosaic work dealing with acts of martyrdom, and the Translation and Recovery of the Body of the Lord. When stray beams of sunlight find their way through the openings in the domes and pass along the gold background, lighting up in odd places small portions of these wonderful *tesseræ* pictures, the effect is very beautiful. All the angles of this mosaic work are rounded off and the travelling rays glinting first on one golden corner, then on another, are strangely attractive to eyes accustomed to the greater architectural severity of a northern clime. The well-chosen slabs that line the lower portions of the cathedral walls have taken to themselves a sombre, dusky hue, a pale velvety brown, but there can be no doubt that in their pristine state they realised in their splendour the Venetian's love of colour.

The strange pulpit, which with part of the rood screen seen in the illustration stands to the north of the steps leading into the presbytery, is arranged in a double tier, and is entered by a double winding stair from the vestibule of the Capella de S. Pietro. Its curious domed sounding-board is very reminiscent of the East. Mention has already been made of the chapels of the Miraculous Virgin and S. Leonard. That dedicated to S. Peter is behind this pulpit on the north side of the presbytery. It has a door leading out into the piazza. The corresponding chapel to the south is dedicated to S. Clement. At the end of the north transept is another to S. Isidore—a dark, solemn little place. The sacristy is beyond the chapel of S. Peter at the back of the presbytery. It is a fine apartment with mosaics from designs by Titian and his pupils, which may be studied as a good example of Renaissance decoration in *tesseræ*. Sansovino, who executed the beautiful door, is said to have had it in hand for twenty years.

The baptistery is entered from the south aisle, and with the adjoining Cappella Zeno is one of the most interesting parts of S. Mark's. In the former is the monument and sarcophagus of Doge Andrea Dandolo, who died in 1354. It is a grand specimen of the sculpture of the age. The recumbent figure of the Doge, who was the last to be buried in S. Mark's, is very serene in its realisation of the Last Sleep. All the mosaics the chamber contains were given and paid for by Andrea. Most of them naturally relate to the Holy Rite. The font is very ancient, and has a fine bronze cover designed by Sansovino and surmounted by a statuette of S. John the Baptist. A very beautiful low relief of four crossed swords which compose a cross, with birds beneath, is let into one of the walls. On the vaulted roof of the Cappella Zeno, the life of the Evangelist, whose body at first rested here, is well depicted in a series of mosaics. The centre of the chapel is occupied by the tomb of Cardinal Zeno, who left the bulk of his immense fortune to S. Mark's. The altar stands under a bronze canopy covering figures of Our Lady (who wears a gilded shoe), S. Peter, and S. John the Baptist. The legend runs that the Virgin gave her bronze shoe once to a poor votary and it was immediately turned into gold. From this incident the chapel, which became the Cardinal's Mausoleum, is also known as that of the Madonna della Scarpa.

Venice possesses nearly seventy churches, but of these only the two most celebrated can be mentioned in this chapter. They are SS. Giovanni e Paolo, and the Frari. The former had its origin in the great preaching Order of S. Dominic, and the latter in that of S. Francis. These saints, bound by vows of poverty, went forth preaching humility, and so great a meed of success did they attain, that we find throughout the country, as a result of their crusade, huge churches like these built to hold large congregations. In Venice both Orders had their following among different patrician families, who were mainly responsible for the monetary assistance the Orders received, and who therefore acquired a sort of prescriptive right to burial space within the holy walls they had helped to raise. For this reason the tombs we find in SS. Giovanni e Paolo and the Frari are not only an epitome of the rulers of Venice, but in them can be traced from the earliest Gothic the different styles of Venetian decorative art as exemplified in her sepulchral monuments.

SS. Giovanni e Paolo is a fine brick building of early Italian Gothic, which was commenced in 1246 and finished in 1390. Its length is three hundred and thirty feet, its width at the transepts one hundred and forty-three, and in the nave ninety-one feet. From this it will be seen that the transepts are short. The spacious nave has five bays, the arches of which are supported by single columns of grey stone with simple floral capitals. The vaulting, as is usual in Italian Gothic, is low. The galleried triforium has small outlets into the church, and a clerestory of pointed lights in groups of three has taken the place of much larger single windows. The aisles are narrow. The apsidal choir is architecturally very striking. From a few feet above the floor rise the long narrow windows of the apse reaching up beyond the base of the vaulting and giving an idea of immense height. The glass they contain is, however, very crude; and, unfortunately, a terrible pink wash covers the walls, so pink that the beauty of the architectural features is considerably marred. The choice of material and the selection of colour has more to do with the success or failure of a building than is generally realised. The transepts, nave, and aisles are coloured grey, and harmonise with the stone columns mentioned above, and with the monuments of faintly tinted marble which crowd the walls of the aisles.

Among the most notable tombs are those of the Mocenigo family, a family which possessed the whole of the west wall of the church, and whose monuments almost cover it. Of the three equestrian tombs that are in the church, pride of place must be given to the one put there to Niccolo Orsini, who commanded the Republic's forces in the war against the League of Cambray. The gilded group of the general and his horse above the sarcophagus is full of life and vigour. The simple but very beautiful tomb of Paolo Loudan, on which his recumbent figure in full chain mail lies stretched, is a fine work of the middle of the fourteenth century.

The grand monument to Andrea Vendramin, who died in 1478, and who was the first of the new nobility to be elevated to the position of sovereign, is the most refined example of a Renaissance tomb in Venice. The Doge lies, with face turned towards the spectator, on a couch supported by eagles. Behind him are pages and other attendants. The carving and arabesques of the canopy and its supports, into which notes symbolical of naval power are crowded, though extremely intricate, are very pure in style. In the lunette beneath the arch kneels the Doge, who is being recommended to Our Lady by S. Mark. Opposite to this beautiful tomb is the Gothic memorial to Doge Michele Morosini, who died in 1382. The background of the central portion is a good mosaic of the Crucifixion, in front of which the aquiline features of the recumbent Duke are very prominent. The niches on either side are filled with figures of different saints, and the whole is surmounted by S. Michael with the Dragon.

The exterior of the church, especially the apse, which rises without a single buttress, is very impressive. A good Gothic portal occupies the centre of the unfinished west façade, which is flanked by thirteenth-century sarcophagi let into niches in the walls. Close by, and occupying one side of the Campo in which the church stands, is the Scuola di S. Marco. This building, now a hospital, was erected in 1485 by Martino Lombardi, and is noteworthy for the curiously conceived façade that faces the square. This is composed of richly coloured marble divided into panels, on which in low relief different buildings are seen in acute perspective. They recall the same sort of decoration which prevails in the frescoes at Pompeii, but so cleverly did Lombardi arrange his scheme that their absolute falsity in no way detracts from the general design of the building.

In front of the façade stands the magnificent equestrian statue to that prince of *condottieri* whose mausoleum at Bergamo has already been mentioned, Bartolommeo Colleoni. A man amongst men, stern, defiant and resourceful, his grand figure embodies all that a leader in troublous times should be. Firmly gripping his saddle, he sits his horse with head thrown back and a face which betokens the masterful haughtiness of the man. The group was designed by Leonardo da Vinci's master, Andrea Verrocchio, and finished by Alessandro Leopardi. It vies with Donatello's equestrian group of Gattamelata at Padua in being perhaps the best Italian Renaissance statue extant.

The Frari is a church which grew out of the accumulated funds of the Franciscans, whose enormous monastery, now holding the municipal archives, adjoins it. This great church was commenced in 1250 and finished in 1338, and contains the monuments and tombs of some of the city's rulers, as well as many of the Venetian nobility who in bygone days made their names famous in its annals. The west façade has a simple Gothic doorway and four round windows, one of which, larger than the others, is above the figure of Christ that occupies the apex of the arch. Like SS. Giovanni e Paolo the east end is architecturally the most interesting part of the fabric. Two flights of lofty windows with exceedingly good tracery admit light into the apse. This has been continued south by later additions as far as the wall of the transept. The transept being thus enlarged has four apsidal chambers that form a pleasing sequence to the big eastern apse. The exterior of the church, when viewed from the little Campo S. Rocco outside the east end, composes extremely well. The four small apses lead up to the big one, behind which and beyond the roof line one sees the great Campanile rising over the north transept. The Frari is built of brick with a simple decorative feature in the form of a course of Venetian Gothic at the top.

Owing to subsidence of the foundations the interior is now undergoing extensive repair. The nave is very lofty, with single columns of grey stone that have floral capitals. The groining ribs of the vault are of red brick and the arches of the bays are grey stone. Two of the nave columns are massively constructed of brick, and form with the brick walls of the aisles and the grey colour of the stone a very charming scheme. The choir occupies the last two bays of the nave, and as is the case in the cathedrals of Spain, is cut off from the body of the church by a rood screen. The portion of this which is in the nave is debased Renaissance, but that in the aisles is earlier and much better. The choir stalls are very finely carved and decorated with superb *intarsia* work. The little door by which the canons enter the choir is particularly good in this respect, with a beauty much enhanced by the design on the doorposts. Round these cling vines and grape clusters. The clerestory consists of round windows with double lights, but there is no triforium. Among the most interesting monuments are those erected to Beato Pacifico, the Franciscan architect of the church, which is in the south transept, and one to Titian in the south aisle. His masterpiece of the Assumption, now in the Accademia delle Belle Arti, was painted for the Frari.

The domestic architecture of Venice is far more interesting than that with which we have just dealt. Peculiar to Venetia, it is the outcome of that period when, the city's trade being well established in northern climes, new ideas and fashions travelled back from countries over the great mountain chain and began to commingle with the older traditions of the East. Not only on the Grand Canal, but in many of the quiet byways of the Silent City, one comes across beautiful examples of that entrancing style of façade, the Venetian Gothic.

As the gondola glides swiftly over the waters of the great highway of Venice there comes into sight a group of palaces which occupies the only real angle of the Grand Canal. This group is formed of the celebrated houses built by the Foscari and Giustiniani families, and is somewhat in the style of the Doge's Palace, the first-named being contemporary with it. The flat brick façades are broken by rows of elegant windows, some with, some without balconies. The deeply-recessed arcading of the central lights of the first and second storeys gives just the right amount of shade to an otherwise flat surface, which the windows above and at either side only slightly relieve. A course of white marble edging and heavy foundations of enormous blocks of the same give solidity, and most beautifully frame the pale-red brick of which the Venetians were so fond. Rows of *pali*, or posts, painted with the colours of the owner, serve as a dock for waiting gondolas. The water of the canal, never quiescent, is a puzzle for the painter who would study reflections. The tide ebbs and flows on the great highway, the convenient but hideous steamboat rushes by, gondolas groan and creak against their moorings, and a kaleidoscope of ever-changing shapes and colours well-nigh drives him to despair.

Figure 13: THE PALAZZI FOSCARI E GIUSTINIANI, VENICE

THE PALAZZI FOSCARI E GIUSTINIANI, VENICE

Further up the Grand Canal is a very ornate palace, the Ca d'Oro, with angles softened by three twisted columns instead of the more usual one in this type of building. Its façade was designed by Giovanni and Bartolommeo Buon, who built the Piazzetta in front of the Doge's Palace. At one time it was entirely covered with gilt—hence the name. Down near the Salute, where the canal opens out to the sea, are the Palazzo da Mula and the fascinating little Palazzo Contarini-Fasan, with its lovely traceried balconies. These are all Venetian Gothic. Of other styles the Byzantine Palazzi, da Mosto and Loudan, the latter Byron's Venetian home, and the Renaissance Palazzi, Rezzonico, where Browning lived, Camerlanghi, Manzoni, with a frieze of eagles, Pesaro, and Dario, with plaques of coloured marble on its façade, are the most celebrated. Most of them are cracking and bulging, and more than one owes its present existence to the iron clamps which hold it together. It is much to be feared that the utilitarian steamboat and ever-increasing motor-boat traffic will sooner or later be responsible for the destruction of many a beautiful building, the foundations of which were never intended to withstand the strain of the great extra wash it creates.

In a safer position than most is the Doge's Palace, that magnificent construction which almost distracts attention from S. Mark's by its side.

The first building to be constructed for the rulers of Venice stood on the site of the Palace and was erected in 813. Fire subsequently destroyed it and also the edifice which replaced the smoking ruins. The present building was commenced in 1301 and save for the outer walls was almost gutted in 1574 and 1577. Palladio, the foremost architect of the day, contended that it would be dangerous to attempt any reconstruction unless these walls were demolished, and it speaks volumes for the good taste of the Senate that his scheme for pulling them down and putting up another palace in his own hard classic style was not adopted. The exterior as we see it is almost entirely due to the talented family of Buon—Giovanni, the father, and his two sons, Pantaleone and Bartolommeo. It is, however, much to be regretted that while restoring the façades this celebrated family of *tajapieri*, or stonecutters, did not adhere to the level and beautiful design of the two windows which escaped the fire at the east end of the façade that looks over the Riva degli Schiavoni out to sea. The short massive columns of the lower colonnade give an idea of immense strength to the great flat space above. The capitals of these stunted columns are extremely interesting. The Virtues and Vices find places amidst their foliage, as do the most famous of Rome's Emperors and Philosophers, the signs of the Zodiac and many other symbols. Twisted shafts, one of the types of Venetian Gothic, terminate the three angles of the upper part of the two façades. Their bases are composed of sculptured groups. The angle nearest to S. Mark's has the Archangel Michael with the Judgment of Solomon below him. The next, at the south-west corner, is a group of Adam and Eve with Gabriel above. In the last, Noah, drunk with wine, is being covered by two of his sons, and above them is S. Raphael with Tobias, who holds a fish.

A noble window and pierced balcony of early fifteenth-century work occupies the centre of the upper arcade which faces the sea. This beautiful window and marble balcony open out from the great Sala Maggiore Consiglio. Above the moulding of the window is a figure of Justice, and below in flanking niches are SS. Peter, Paul and Mark; Faith, Hope and Charity; and the four Cardinal Virtues. A fine loggia, with cusped arches and quatrefoils above, runs round both the exposed sides of the Palace. The plan of the building is an irregular square with a great courtyard inside. The courtyard is Renaissance, the east side being a particularly good example of a period when the wealth of Venice was lavished on her buildings.

In the north-east corner of this court and opposite to the Porta della Carta, is the famous Scala dei Giganti, erected by Rizzio in 1483. At the head of this magnificent Staircase of the Giants, the Doges were crowned with the Cap of Authority. From it an open corridor runs right and left. On the right the Scala d'Oro ascends to the second floor. Only those whose names were inscribed in the Libro d'Oro were permitted to use this stairway, which led to that portion of the Palace occupied by the Doges and their attendant nobles. The continuous suite of magnificent apartments through which the visitor wanders seem full of emptiness and sadly want the stately figures and quaint dress, the sonorous voices and courtly manners of the bygone age that once peopled them and made them live. The gorgeously gilded and coloured ceilings become not only oppressive from their magnificence, but wearisome by their repetition; and despite the great traditions that cling to the Palace and the remembrance of the history made within these chambers, it is with a sigh of relief that one steps out on to the balcony where Justice holds the Scales above our head, and drinks in the balmy air that floats in over the lagoons keeping Venice pure and sweet.

Figure 14: THE LION OF S. MARK'S, VENICE

THE LION OF S. MARK'S, VENICE

Outside on the Riva at the end of the Piazzetta are two columns of granite that were brought to Venice in 1180 by Doge Michiel. One came from Syria, the other from Constantinople. On the capital of one is the Winged Lion of S. Mark, the emblem of Venice's patron saint; an emblem which is to be found in every city in the country that owned allegiance to the Doge's rule. On the other is a figure of S. Theodore, who stands over a crocodile. S. Theodore, it will be remembered, was the tutelary saint of Venice before his deposition on the arrival of S. Mark's body; but this statue was not put up on the monolith until the year 1329. These two great columns look across the water to the isle of S. Giorgio Maggiore, where Palladio's great church stands in its chilly splendour. Beyond are the lagoons and the open sea. The marble-paved landing-stage on which they stand is from one point of view the most interesting part of Venice. On it her great traders and merchants gathered when the long-expected ships from the East came into sight; and as they swept proudly up the channels and dropped anchor opposite, one can well imagine the excitement of the thankful owners who would in a few minutes go on board and learn of the success or failure of the long voyage just ended.

The oldest part of Venice lies across the Rialto bridge, on the island of Rivo Alto, where the fish and vegetable markets now are. As this little town grew more prosperous a wooden bridge, replaced in 1588 by the present one, was built to connect Rivo Alto with the island opposite; and by degrees the seventy-two islands on which the city is built became absorbed within her borders. It must never be forgotten that Venice, until connected with the mainland by a railway bridge, always faced the sea, which, as Grant Allen writes, was the front door.

Long before the Venice of Rivo Alto came into being, there was a flourishing little city not many miles away on the island of Torcello. At the time when Attila and his Huns descended on the Roman colony of Aquileia and wrought devastation throughout that flourishing outpost of the world's greatest city, many of the inhabitants, leaving their desolate homes to the mercy of the invader, fled to the swamps and islands at the estuaries of the rivers Po, Adige, and Brenta. Amidst these dismal surroundings the greater number found refuge on the island of Torcello. From Torcello the refugees in time pushed out to the surrounding islands, and an important station was established on Rivo Alto. Thus began Venice; and from this little island grew that great Republic, the Mistress of the Seas, which down to the time of the French Revolution had never seen a conquering host enter its waterways.

As early as 641 Torcello possessed a cathedral. This was rebuilt in 874, and parts of the structure were later on incorporated into the building which stands to-day just as it did when finished in the early eleventh century by Bishop Orseolo. Its architectural interest lies in its being an Italian church on strict Byzantine lines, and it is one of the earliest examples of cultivated native art. Its exterior possesses the simplicity of all early work and stands up like a great barrack, with its *campanile* a landmark for miles over the dreary waste of waters. The interior is very austere and cold. The bays on either side of the nave separate it from the aisles. The columns that support the round arches are a light grey marble; the capitals, Corinthianized Byzantine. The clerestory lights, which are placed just under the roof, are on the south side only, those on the north having been blocked up at some remote period. The south aisle is lit by narrow round-headed windows, each of which has a great marble shutter slab on the outside still swinging in its marble socket—a reminiscence of Ancient Rome, and one that exists in the Roman butchers' shops of to-day. A rood-screen shuts off the choir, the four panels of it facing the nave are particularly fine examples of the art of the early eleventh century. The two centre panels have each a couple of peacocks with necks outstretched feeding on foliage; and in the two outer two lions are sculptured in perspective, a rather unusual thing for so early a work. These panels support six elegant columns, which in their turn hold a series of painted panels of wood of the fourteenth century on which the Madonna and twelve Apostles are represented. A very fine pulpit, with reading-desk below, is to the north of the screen. It has an interesting bas-relief at the base, reconstructed in the twelfth century.

Behind the high altar, under which rest the remains of S. Eliodorus, is the tribune. This part of the church is unique. The apse is arranged in eight semicircular rows of seats, occupied at one time by the lesser clergy, in the centre of which, elevated to a position just under the small eastern light, is the bishop's throne. The throne is approached by a dozen steps separated from the rows of seats by a marble wall. The seats in times gone by were white marble, but have been recently restored and are now of brick. Despite their present warm colour, the damp chilliness of this beautiful little church strikes a mournful note hardly relieved by the flaring red brick, or the gorgeous tone of the mosaics which cover the vaulting of the choir and apse.

In the semi-dome of the apse a dignified Madonna and Child gaze serenely below, with white-robed Apostles ranged round. The mosaics, however, which cover the west wall are of greater artistic interest, being of the ninth century. They illustrate the narrative of early Christian tradition and are divided into five bands carrying out its ideas. The marvellous tessellated floor of the cathedral has withstood, in a wonderful manner, the damp and ravages of time, but, like that of S. Mark's, is very uneven. There is an air of decay and long oblivion about the whole building that nothing can efface.

Outside, and joined to the cathedral by a cloistered walk, is the church of Sta. Fosca. Originally a basilica of the ninth century, this much dilapidated little edifice was rebuilt in 1008 in the shape of a Greek cross. A rotunda occupies the centre, inside which runs a grey pillared arcade built to support a dome that was never constructed. There are three apses; the middle one has two rows of blind arcading with ornamental brickwork above. A brick loggia, covered with whitewash, is outside, and connects with the cloister and the cathedral. Sta. Fosca suffered martyrdom at Ravenna her native city, and her remains were brought here, and this now damp ruinous little church built around them.

On the green grass of the little piazza, which one can hardly realise was once the focus of a thriving city, stands an ancient stone chair called "The Throne of Attila." It most probably was used at the inauguration ceremony of Torcello's chief magistrates. A column of later date is beside it, and behind them, occupying one side of this deserted square, is the Palazzo del Commune, a building of the thirteenth century, now used as the museum wherein are gathered all the relics of Torcello's ancient glory that time unearths. As the gondola carries one back to Venice it threads deserted canals, and passes under many a bridge the voussoirs of which are the only remaining stones of structures that spanned the water and connected the islands over which a populous civilisation spread itself. Save for the "quack" of an occasional duck hidden in the reeds of the marsh and the garrulity of the gondolier all is silence and solitude. A vast sky above but adds to the feeling of desolation, as, level with the water's edge, we skim along. Who can tell whether Venice herself one day may not become what fascinating though dreary Torcello now is!

Figure 15: S. FOSCA AND CATHEDRAL, TORCELLO

S. FOSCA AND CATHEDRAL, TORCELLO

RIMINI

IT is not every visitor to Rome who, passing under the Porta del Popolo and seeing in front a straight road with a row of squalid dwellings on one side, knows that that road, the old Via Flaminia, terminates on the Adriatic coast at far-off Rimini. This, the great highway out of Rome northwards, enters Rimini under the noble Arch of Augustus, a very fine gateway built of *travertine*. Passing through the market-place named the Piazza Giulio Cesare—for here stands a pedestal with the legend that from it Julius Cæsar harangued his troops after the crossing of the Rubicon—it runs on and out of the city over the bridge that crosses the river Marrecchia. This bridge, which was commenced during the reign of Augustus and finished by Tiberius, is one of the best preserved in Italy. Of its five arches, that in the centre has the greatest span, and the two which flank it are a little larger than those at either end. Traces of pediments may still be seen on its massive buttresses. The parapet is capped by a rounded stone course. From the two central piers inwards and over the arch this course is raised to a higher level than on the remainder of the bridge. In summer a shallow little river meanders in silvery threads over the pebbles which form the almost dry bed of the stream, and finds its way under the arches into the harbour half a mile beyond. In winter a rushing torrent has for centuries beaten against the piers that the workmen of Augustus' time laid so well. The road above, no longer the Via Flaminia but now the Via Æmilia, runs out over the plain in a north-westerly direction to Rome's ancient colonies in the province from which it derives its name. Many fragments and columns, let into the walls and forming part of the building material of the houses of Rimini, are evidence of its importance in the days of the early emperors. Those were days when it formed with Pesaro, Fano, Sinigallia and Ancona, the group known as the five "Maritime Cities," and was one of the Capital's great Adriatic ports. The sea is but a mile off and the level sands of Rimini nowadays attract hundreds of summer visitors who take advantage of their unrivalled bathing facilities.

The first bishop was appointed to Ariminium as early as 260, and ninety-nine years later the celebrated council of the Arians and Athanasians met to deliberate over their differences in the city. In the sixteenth century, when it formed part of Otho III.'s empire, a Malatesta was appointed viceroy of Le Marche, and the long connection of this family with Rimini then commenced. The most renowned member of the "Wrong-heads" was undoubtedly Sigismondo, a man of great ferocity of disposition and licentious in his habits. Like many another bellicose noble, Sigismondo had two sides to his nature, and whatever his faults, it is to his credit that many of his leisure hours were spent in the company of philosophers and men of pacific tastes. It is due to his patronage of Art that the genius of Leo Battista Alberti, another curious and complex product of the age, found scope in the great church of S. Francesco. We owe to these two men—one the patron, the other the architect—the best example of transition from Gothic to Renaissance which Italy possesses.

The cathedral, a Gothic edifice dedicated to S. Francesco, was but one hundred years old when Sigismondo set Alberti to work on its transformation. Malatesta undoubtedly intended it to be the mausoleum of his race, and that is what this most unecclesiastical building, which is called the Tempio di Malatesta, is. The façade is extremely simple. It is spaced out into three equal divisions. The centre is occupied by the portal which has a good pediment and a round arch borne by highly ornate pilasters. On either side are four Corinthian columns supporting the three flat-membered arches of the façade. Over them is a broad frieze. The bases of these columns stand on a very beautiful course which is continued round the two sides of the Tempio. At intervals, amidst finely-chiselled heraldic roses and little elephants, are alternating shields bearing the I and S of Isotta and Sigismondo—initials that are found in every available place throughout the building—and the coat of arms of the Malatesta.

On the north and south sides of the building a grand row of seven broad round arches, on massive rectangular piers, throws a deep shadow on to the sarcophagi of the men who were Sigismondo's companions in his peaceful hours. These sarcophagi are placed between the piers, well above the spectator, on the basement which is built out from the brick wall of the original Gothic cathedral. Like the façade, this grand colonnade and its base are lined with white marble. Among the sarcophagi is one which contains a trophy brought by Sigismondo from the East.

The civilisation of the Middle Ages produced a curious phase of religion that showed itself not only in the Church, which distributed the bodies of Christian martyrs all over the country and robbed the catacombs of Rome for sacred relics in order that they might be adored in other places, but also in the action of the great nobles, who, to gain a little immortality, brought back from distant wars all they could lay hands on that might redound to their heavenly credit. In the case of Sigismondo it was, let us believe, a love of literature that prompted the theft of the bones of the great Platonist, Gemisthus Pletho, and placed them in the stone chest under one of Alberti's arches. There they rest near those containing the remains of kindred natures whom the warlike noble claimed as intimate friends.

The interior of the Tempio consists of a nave with side chapels and an apsidal choir. The roof is good open woodwork. There are four chapels on either side with the original pointed vault and groining. The Gothic arches which open on to the nave are covered with classic ornament. The spandrils are coloured green and are embossed with shields and a splendid floral design. The wall spaces between each chapel, as well as the west end, have a wonderful arrangement of very beautiful Corinthian pilasters that rest on a sculptured frieze with a blue ground on which are shields bearing the I and S. From this frieze depend floral festoons on bands of green and red, with medallions of coloured marble beneath. At the bases of the pilasters are figures holding shields. The whole of this design is executed in a grey stone of the same colour as that in the illustration. The piers of the arches of the two first chapels on either side are enriched by figures of knights and dames; the third by beautiful panels of nymphs and children carrying garlands, &c., on a light blue ground reminiscent of the Della Robbia. The fourth chapel on the south side has figures symbolical of the months of the year and the signs of the Zodiac; while that on the north has figures of saints on its piers, to which, instead of the usual classic bases, elephants of black marble have been substituted. The first chapel south is dedicated to S. Sigismondo, who sits on two of these great beasts. The Malatesta crest is above the altar. On one wall are delicately carved figures of angels drawing aside curtains from a crucifix; repeated on another, where the angels in even better attitudes part the curtains from a small closed window that looks into the Sanctuario. So delicately cut are these beautiful figures that the art which produced them seems almost plastic. The Sanctuario is closed and contains a fresco of Sigismondo Malatesta kneeling before his patron saint. The next chapel appears in the illustration. It is dedicated to S. Michele, whose figure above the altar is supposed to be a portrait of Isotta. She is interred in the tomb which the sketch shows. During the life of Sigismondo's two wives she was his mistress, but at the death of the second he married her and the record of their wedded life is a happy one. Her tomb is borne by elephants on brackets and is surmounted by a knight's helm with the Malatesta crest above.

Figure 16: ISOTTA'S TOMB IN THE CATHEDRAL, RIMINI

ISOTTA'S TOMB IN THE CATHEDRAL, RIMINI

The first chapel on the north side of the nave has a tomb placed high up on the wall, which contains the remains of as many of Sigismondo's least famous ancestors as he could lay hands on. The chapel is known as the Capella dell' Acque from an ancient statue of the Madonna which represents her as sending down rain. On the base of the pillars of this chapel are portraits in low relief of Sigismondo. The low brow, hooked nose, and cruel mouth tell one plainly that the sardonic expression of the face does not belie the character of this extraordinary man. On the wall to the right of the west door is his tomb, which, considering the part he played in the history of his day, must be acknowledged as very simple and plain.

The other chapels are full of the tombs of the illustrious members, male and female, of the House of Malatesta.

Along the length of the nave in front of all these chapels runs a splendid marble screen or balustrade. At every fourth pillar, on the marble rail, stands a charming little cherub resting on a shield or holding a bunch of flowers or basket of fruit. The screen of the last chapel on each side is of red Verona marble and is perforated by the elephant head of the Malatesta and gorgeously designed arabesques in circles. From one end to the other the screens stand out from the chapels into the nave, and are raised two steps above the red-tiled floor. Such are some of the features which go to make the Tempio di Malatesta one of the most extraordinary cathedrals in Italy.

There is little else to attract the visitor to Rimini, unless it be to undertake a visit to the tiny Republic of S. Marino. A pleasant day's excursion may be taken to this quaint little stretch of territory which is so picturesquely situated on a spur of the Alban mountains a few miles from the city.

FERRARA

AT the foot of the Euganean hills, those hills which stand like sentinels detached from the northern ramparts of Venetia, and guarding the tract of country that stretches eastwards to the sea between Rovigo and Venice, are the ruins of a castle—the Castello d'Este—whose lords at one time played a prominent part in the history of Italy. Of Lombard origin, these Margraves of Este had ruled the surrounding country for three centuries prior to 1452, in which year Pope Paul III. created Borso d'Este Duke of Ferrara, and the family, as long as it lasted, was thenceforth inseparably connected with the subject of this chapter. More honours were bestowed on Borso when the Emperor Frederick III. gave him the titles of Duke of Modena and Reggio, and he held the domains of those places as fiefs for his overlord. Borso's grandson Alphonso married the notorious Lucrezia Borgia; but to Azzo d'Este, Margrave of Este in the year 1110, belongs a greater claim to fame. Scion of a junior branch of the Welfs or Guelphs he succeeded to the Duchy of Bavaria on the death of his grandfather, the last male representative of the elder branch of the family, and from his off-spring grew the Guelph Houses of Hanover and Brunswick, from the former of which is descended our own Royal line. In the sixteenth century the Court of Ferrara was second to none in Europe for its patronage of the Arts and Literature, and the House of Este will always be handed down to posterity as one that did much to raise the culture of Italy to a very high pitch.

In the centre of the city, surrounded by a moat and entered by two bridges which span it, the great pile that Ferrara's rulers erected stands haughtily four-square, with four immense towers at the corners. Here in safety dwelt those mighty princes who brought renown to the city that lay around and beyond; and here in a dungeon below the level of the water, Duke Niccolo III. caused his wife and her paramour, who was one of his own natural sons, to be put to death; a tragedy which gave Byron his subject in the poem "Parisina." This huge fortress, like most of the other buildings in Ferrara, is constructed of brick. Ferrara's streets are wide, and though its palaces and houses do not rise to any great height, the gardens behind them, enclosed by high walls, give an air of spaciousness and aristocratic bearing that attest its former importance. Most of these palaces and houses are decorated with beautifully moulded brick or terra cotta courses; and the well-proportioned windows on their flat street fronts create the impression of great space, which is the chief characteristic of Ferrara. There is one important building, however, which is constructed of stone, the Palazzo de' Diamanti, so called from the peculiar facets of the material with which it is built. Ferrara possessed a school of painting of its own, and it is in this palace that the best examples have been placed. The great palace of the Bentivoglio family, where many celebrities have lodged, has a heavy stone cornice and baroque decoration on its vast brick sides. The Casa di Ariosto, built by the poet himself in the years 1526-28, and in which he died, with an inscription on its walls he composed, is another fine house. The hospital of Sta Anna, a most beautiful red brick and terra cotta building, has cloistered courts; and the cellar which was Tasso's prison for five months until he was removed, still a prisoner, to a better room, can be seen. In the *castello* itself Calvin the reformer found an asylum, befriended by Renée, the wife of Duke Ercole d'Este, who paid forfeit for her temerity by being separated from husband and children by a Papal Bull.

The Cathedral was begun in 1135, and its exterior belongs almost entirely to that period. The west façade is a very good example of Lombardo Gothic. It is divided into three equal portions each of which is surmounted by a gable containing what was at one time a wheel window. The central part has a good porch somewhat similar in design to the one at Verona. The semicircular arch is borne by columns supported by two dwarf figures bent double with the weight of their burden; they squat on the backs of lions, one of which holds a bull and the other a ram between its forepaws. Above this is an open gallery with very beautiful twisted pillars and quatrefoil piercing in the three arches. In the spandrils of these, and of earlier date, are bas-reliefs of the dead rising from their tombs, and over them at the base of the canopy above are reliefs of the Life of Our Saviour, the Virtues, the Vices and Seven Mortal Sins, as well as the Day of Judgment. The two flanking parts of the façade, one of which appears in the illustration, have each three tiers of arcading. The lowest is composed of nine rounded arches with four-sided columns grouped in triplets, which are enclosed by three pointed arches. The next tier is of nine pointed arches; and over this are four pointed arches deeply recessed. Following the line of the gable is an extremely effective gallery of elegant double columns and pointed arches, one of the great features of Pisan Gothic so prominent in the churches of Lucca. Near the base of this wall in a curious pilgrim's dress with a pleated skirt is the figure of Alberto d'Este.

Figure 17: THE CATHEDRAL, FERRARA

THE CATHEDRAL, FERRARA

The whole of the south wall has a double range of arches which very pleasantly break the monotony of so vast a space of yellow brick. The grand *campanile* at the south east-corner was put up by Ercole II., and is composed of four tiers of round arches on columns with Corinthian capitals. The alternate bands of red and cream toned marble with which the exterior is faced give a good decorative effect to this big tower.

The interior of the Cathedral has been modernised and painted to represent carved stone. Whitewash, generally the alternative to painted imitation of something substantial in construction, is perhaps preferable to this form of deception as it does not really interfere with the proportions of the architect's design. Here, however, the really fine proportion of the interior is almost destroyed by the obtrusive colours of the false marble walls, and the representation of bosses and capitals. The semicircular choir by Rossette was built in 1499 and has a ceiling covered with a fresco of the Last Judgment by Bastianino, who was one of Michael Angelo's favourite pupils. This fresco contains portraits of many of the painter's friends who are depicted in Heaven, while those with whom he was not on good terms are enduring the tortures of another place.

In the piazza outside the Cathedral a market goes on all day long throughout the year. It is difficult to analyse the feelings of folk who in the bitterest of weather unfold their great umbrellas over the fruit and vegetables exposed for sale. But so it is in Ferrara during November when the accompanying sketch was made, and every morning sees a thick coat of ice on the moat surrounding the castle. For although the good people wrapped themselves in heavy cloaks and thick coats and shivered over charcoal stoves, they still sat under their umbrellas. Habit breeds custom and custom lasts for ages.

The old city walls afford a delightful promenade of four miles or more in length. On one side, the town seems to be right in the middle of a huge market garden above the trees of which long red roofs and towers rise upwards. On the other, at this time of year, the last leaves from rows of poplars and plane trees may be seen gently falling to the ground in the tranquil frosty air, and when at rest forming a glorious carpet of russet and orange. Great teams of oxen, six couple to a team, are straining hard at the plough that cuts deep furrows in the stiff soil. The trees have long ago been trimmed and the peasants now turn their hands to the cutting of clay—that stiff clay through which the oxen toil—for brick-making. Ice covers the water in the fosse, and although the sun shines brilliantly and the malarial mosquito is no more for at least eight months, one soon realises that Ferrara is better in the spring than in late autumn.

RAVENNA

RAVENNA is one of those ancient cities the origin of which is lost in the mist of ages. It is, however, no guess work to say that in the days before the first unknown settlers found their way to the spot which became their permanent home, the fertile land in which it now lies embowered was a vast waste of waters and salt marshes. The first inhabitants of this dreary region drove piles into the mud, and erected their dwellings on such foundations as these afforded. Wooden piles will not last for ever, and the subsequent buildings that were put up, pulled down and replaced, have accordingly suffered in stability. When the march of Rome carried her legions north, Ravenna was encircled by a seagirt wall, and a Roman colony was established which became in Pompey's day a first-class naval station. Alive to the great strategic value of the city the Emperor Augustus constructed a new and second harbour capable of holding two hundred and fifty ships, which he named Portus Classis. This he connected by a canal with one of the estuaries of the river Po. Portus Classis lay three miles south of Ravenna, and between the two there soon sprang up a connecting link, the town of Cæsarea. The Emperor Honorius made Ravenna the capital of the West, and both he and his celebrated sister Placidia resided there.

In 493 Theodoric, king of the Ostrogoths, who had extended his conquests southwards over the Alps, captured the city, and Ravenna then became the capital of the Gothic kingdom. During his reign, a reign marked by absolute religious toleration, Italy was at peace for thirty years. Ravenna must have been at that time some miles from the coast. Jordanes, the historian, has handed down the fact that its celebrated Pineta, or Pine Forest, was in existence in Theodoric's day. Justinian, who drove out the Goths with the help of Belisarius and Narses, left the administration in the hands of the latter, who became the first Exarch. The Exarchs of Ravenna practically governed the entire Italian kingdom; even the Popes were subject to a rule which lasted one hundred and eighty-five years. In 1512 the Italian war that followed the League of Cambray brought a French army under Gaston le Foix into Romagna, and the bloodiest battle ever fought on Italian soil took place not far from the city; Gaston losing his life towards the close of the engagement at a spot marked by an obelisk.

It is, however, in early Christian Art, nowhere so well exemplified as in the mosaics of Ravenna, that interest is chiefly centred. More than fourteen centuries have come and gone since the first of these wonderful wall decorations were placed where they remain to-day. And though Ravenna and its celebrated Pine Forest are inseparably connected with the immortal Dante and the poet Byron, and though the sarcophagus and tomb of the former, tucked away in a corner of a little piazza, draw many a pilgrim to worship at his shrine, Ravenna lives in its mosaics and will continue thus to live as long as the walls last on which they are encrusted.

Theodoric's great basilica possesses one that is universally accepted as the finest in the world, but the church of S. Vitale is enriched with the most splendid of all. Close to S. Vitale is the mausoleum which Honorius' sister, Galla Placidia, built in the form of a Latin cross for herself and her husbands. In its way it is one of the most perfect gems of good taste in mural decoration extant. The interior walls are lined with rare marbles. The arch over the entrance has a mosaic of the Good Shepherd and His Sheep in subdued greens and greys. The vault of the first arm of the cross is covered with a most glorious blue ground out of which shines a multitude of stars in white and gold; this leads the eye in a perfect harmony of colour to the blue-green ground of the dome, whereon the four Evangelists and their symbols are portrayed in white and a dull red. The sarcophagus of the Empress still remains in the recess beyond, and in the lateral arms of the cross are those of her brother Honorius and her second husband Constantius III. These three stand exactly in the same places as they did fourteen hundred years ago. The mosaic above Placidia's tomb represents Our Lord with an open book in one hand and a cross in the other. In the centre is a gridiron towards which He proceeds. On the left side a sort of tomb or cupboard stands open disclosing on its shelves the bodies of the four Evangelists, their names being written beneath each body.

In the other recesses stags are seen drinking at fountains, and birds and arabesques cover the beautiful *tesseræ* groundwork. The soffits of all the windows, which are filled with thin slabs of alabaster, are adorned by a deep red, and a black and white pattern on a gold ground.

Figure 18: RAVENNA

RAVENNA

S. Vitale, the building to the right in the sketch, was erected in the reign of Justinian by Archbishop Ecclesius on the spot where S. Vitalis suffered martyrdom. Like most of the early buildings of Ravenna it has suffered from the nature of the ground on which it stands, and is buttressed up and held together by great iron ties and clamps. The interior is a vast circle with a domed roof supported by eight arches and the same number of piers, between which are semicircular two-storied recesses. These are divided by three arches with plain columns that have double capitals. A circular aisle extends round the lower part of the church carrying a gallery above. The brick walls, against which are placed many ancient sarcophagi, were originally covered with slabs of marble, and as S. Vitale and most of Ravenna's other churches are now *monumentali nazionale* it is to be hoped that marble may some day once more line this effective interior.

The superb mosaics on the vault of the Choir and Tribune are of the sixth century, and as fresh to-day as when first put up. The semi-dome of the apse has a fine gold ground on which the Almighty is enthroned on a globe with Archangels around. Above them float crimson and blue clouds. He gives to S. Vitalis, who stands at His right hand, the crown of martyrdom; on His left is S. Eutychius offering a model of the church. The vault of the Tribune itself is decorated with one of the most gorgeous arrangements of colour in arabesques and birds that could be imagined. On one wall is a fine mosaic of Justinian surrounded by courtiers, and S. Maximianus with two accompanying priests. The Emperor's robe is deep purple embroidered with gold and mother-of-pearl, those that the others wear are white and gold with coloured edging. On the opposite wall is the Empress Theodora attended by the ladies of her court. Here again the costumes give a fine colour note, and the expressions on the different faces, which are very Eastern in type, are remarkable. A curtain forms part of the background of this mosaic, and is, curiously enough, green, white and red, the Italian colours of the present day. On the arch are half-lengths of our Saviour and the twelve Apostles, and the two martyred sons of S. Vitalis, SS. Gervasius and Protasius whose remains rest in the church of S. Ambrogio in Milan.

All the angles of the mosaics are rounded off as in S. Mark's at Venice and elsewhere. But in S. Vitale they are patterned with bands of distinct colours, and do not interfere with the general effect as they do in S. Mark's, where the brilliant gold catches the light and accentuates the angle. The whole colour scheme of the decoration is green and white relieved by a dull purple, black and deep red set on a rich dull golden ground. However much one admires the later mosaics of Venice and Torcello, Palermo and Monreale, the palm for beautiful colour must be awarded to the glorious art of Ravenna.

At the bases of the columns in the Choir stand the celebrated pagan bas-reliefs called the "Throne of Neptune." In both, a sea-monster lies extended beneath the throne of the god. That on the right has a winged figure holding a trident; in the other, two figures bear a huge conch shell. Sea-horses, dolphins and shells, crowded in between Corinthian pilasters, form the lower panels which two nude boys bear on their shoulders staggering under the heavy weight.

Ravenna's cathedral contains nothing of any architectural interest, as it was rebuilt in the bad period of the eighteenth century. The original edifice, which was erected by S. Ursus in the fourth century, was known as the "Basilica Ursiana." The Archbishop's Palace adjoins the east end, and in it is one of Ravenna's earliest places of Christian worship. The little chapel to which we refer was probably built about 430 and was the work of Peter Chrysologos. With the exception of painted restorations to some of its frescoes it is to-day just as it was when the decorators left it more than fourteen hundred years ago. In the vestibule leading to the chapel one may see the ivory throne of S. Maximianus. This fine specimen of sixth-century art is covered with little ivory panels on which bas-reliefs tell the history of Joseph. In front of the seat are the Saint's monogram, the panels beneath representing the favourite theme of our Lord as a shepherd amidst his sheep, with the four Evangelists attendant. The four legs of the throne appear to be solid ivory; those at the back go right up to the top and must at one time have been splendid tusks.

To the north of the Cathedral is the Baptistery. The mosaics of the fifth century which line the interior are in a very light key of colour, the scheme employed being light blue, white and gold. Situated between the eight arches of the octagon are sixteen bas-reliefs of the prophets executed in a cream-coloured marble. The arches themselves are composed of two members, one within the other, the outer of which is gold edged with white; and the inner has a remarkably fine quality of blue *tesseræ*. In the centre of the dome

S. John is seen baptizing our Saviour, who stands in the waters of Jordan surrounded by the twelve Apostles. The font, which stands on a fine inverted Corinthian capital, was at one time a vase in the Temple of Jupiter. This Temple was situated on the site of the Baptistery, and eight of its columns form the support of the octagon arches.

The cathedral, which is the church with a dome in the illustration, possesses one of the round towers peculiar to Ravenna. The date of these towers is uncertain, but is probably the eleventh or twelfth century. Insecure foundations have caused most of them to tilt to one side—note the angle of the Torre del Pubblico in the sketch—and necessitated a great deal of restoration.

Theodoric erected his palace and the basilica which adjoins, in the wide thoroughfare that runs north and south from the Porta Serrata to the Porta Nuova. Very little, if anything, remains of the first-named building. And judging from the Romanesque features of a brick colonnade and the portion of a sometime large dwelling that stands behind it, it is very doubtful whether any of the original palace exists. We have it on record, too, that Charles the Great carried off the marble columns of Theodoric's building to adorn his own palace in Aachen; and, as he did this, there is every probability that he took other material as well. But, if we have nothing left of the Gothic king's residence, we have his grand Arian basilica intact. Theodoric dedicated his church to S. Martin, but when the body of S. Apollinaris was deposited in it, a rededication to him took place. S. Apollinare Nuovo, as it has since been called in contradistinction to the other basilica at Classis, is famous throughout Christendom; famous for the finest mosaic in the world. On the north wall, in the blank space where the triforium might be, facing the sun, the Virgin is seen seated on an orange coloured cushion which rests upon a throne. She holds in her lap the Child. Two angels stand on either side. Their robes are white, hers is deep purple fringed with gold and sparkling jewels. Advancing towards her are the Three Kings of the East, whose names appear above each, Melchior, Gaspar and Balthassar. In their hands are silver vessels. The first angel holds his out to receive them. Beyond the kings, in a row, twenty-two virgins come bearing crowns. They are garbed in light purple with white veils; round their waists are bejewelled belts. The expression on the face of each is different, and each is in a slightly different attitude; one is accompanied by a little white dog. They tread lightly on the green sward from which many little flowers lift their humble heads. Between each a palm-tree grows with spreading leaves and clustering dates. It is a wonderful procession. The eagerness and haste of the Three Kings, the dignified and stately rhythm of the slowly pacing Virgins are so well realised, that, although there is no idea of anything but flat decoration in the rendering, a feeling of continuous motion holds one throughout. In the darkened corner at the west end of the mosaic are the walls of the City of Classis. The golden *tesseræ* of these walls are so dark and frowning that they might almost be called brown. Brown they appear to be, but this is because, through an arched opening, three ships with white sails come gliding into port over the cærulean blue of the sea. The eye is thus carried along the whole length of the mosaic without a single jarring note. From the white angels at one end to the white sails at the other, it travels along with a consciousness of repose, and one feels instinctively that one is in the presence of a masterpiece.

Figure 19: S. APOLLINARE NUOVO, RAVENNA

S. APOLLINARE NUOVO, RAVENNA

On the opposite wall, occupying the same position as Classis, are the city of Ravenna and the palace of Theodoric. Corresponding with the two and twenty virgins are figures of twenty-five saints clad in white—save one— and all bearing crowns. Our Saviour, seated between four angels, gives His benediction to the saints, who advance towards Him. The first, in a violet robe, is S. Martinus, the patron of the Church when the sound of the Arian creed filled its aisles. Above both these mosaics are round-headed clerestory windows with saints and prophets in the panels between. The ancient marble throne of the Arian bishops still exists in a little chapel in the north aisle; and here also are some relics of S. Apollinaris.

One of the architectural features of Ravenna's churches may be seen in the double capitals of the columns, which give them a sort of stilt, a peculiarity which does not prevail in churches elsewhere of the same date—the fifth and sixth centuries. Into these two centuries were crowded the great architectural works and their interior decorations that have made Ravenna famous. But it is sad to think that the names of those whose genius found scope on their walls, if ever recorded, have been lost.

The other great basilica, dedicated to S. Apollinaris, S. Apollinare in Classe, stands in solemn loneliness some three miles south of the city. Of Augustus' great port this church, emblem of stability, alone remains. Its round *campanile* towers up over the swampy meadows and uninhabited district that seem given up entirely to the sky and winds. An atrium, now reduced to a portico, stood at one time in front of the façade, but there is nothing to attract one in the barn-like exterior of the building save the glamour attached to its history, which is accentuated by the dreary desolation around.

Inside, the nave is divided by twelve round arches on each side; these are supported by columns of *cipollino* marble. The Byzantine capitals, as in S. Apollinare in Nuovo, are surmounted by an impost with a cross in relief. A fine flight of steps leads up to the High Altar, Choir and Tribune. The crypt is beneath. The floor of the nave, which slopes upwards towards the east, is four feet above the original, which was partly covered with mosaic. A temple of Apollo stood on the site before the church was erected in the year 534, and this older floor may be part of the pagan building.

The mosaics of the Choir and Tribune were undergoing restoration at the time when this was written, but although partly covered up enough was visible to show that in the semi-dome of the apse a large golden cross, with a representation of the Almighty's Head in the centre, occupied the middle of a very brilliant blue circle. The soffit of the arch of the Choir has a blue ground covered with multi-coloured birds and arabesques.

Amongst other of Ravenna's churches the modernised basilica of S. Francesco, the church contiguous to Dante's tomb, contains some ancient sarcophagi and the finest tomb slab in Italy. This is now out of danger and has been placed on the west wall of the nave. It originally covered the remains of Ostasio da Polenta, Lord of Ravenna. He is represented in the garb of a Franciscan friar and lies outstretched, with beautifully modelled hands and face, under a very rich Gothic canopy. The Polenta family were the first to befriend the great poet when he sought refuge here from Florence.

Adjoining the back premises of one of the hotels is the old Arian baptistery, now the oratory of Sta. Maria in Cosmedin. It was here that the first Christian baptism in Ravenna took place. The church of S. Spirito built by Theodoric opens on to the same courtyard; but, next to the Gothic king's great basilica, the most interesting building connected with his name is that which is situated half a mile outside the Porta Serrata.

A pleasant avenue with well-kept rose beds leads one on towards a circular building of grey Istrian limestone, which is covered with a dome of the same material, and we are in the presence of the tomb which Theodoric erected as the resting-place for his mortal remains. We do not see it now as it was when the great king's bones reposed in a sarcophagus within. To the Church of Rome Theodoric was a heretic, and when the Goths were driven out of Ravenna and the Arian ritual was heard no more, the Church ordered the sarcophagus to be broken up, and the ashes of him who was tolerant to all creeds to be scattered to the winds. The tomb was despoiled of its ornaments, and consecrated and used as a chapel. Even now it is sublime in its simplicity, and grand in its massive construction. Its plan is a rotunda resting on a decagonal lower chamber, each side of which is recessed and arched by great blocks of limestone set as the Etruscans set the roofs of their tombs. Rising in two storeys from the ground, which is six feet below the present level of the surrounding orchards, its dome is barely visible above the tops of the fruit trees. The lower storey rests on a platform of stone. Its pavement is always under a few inches of water. The upper storey is reached by two flights of steps which, built outside, give entrance to the sepulchral chamber from a gallery or platform that circulates round the exterior. This gallery formed at one time a portico. The shafts and bases of the colonnade were found buried in the ground when the last restoration took place in 1857. A massive cornice with a circular pattern is on the wall above, and the empty sockets placed at regular intervals, which one sees below it, presumably held the stone that formed the roof. The dome is one huge block of stone estimated to weigh two hundred tons. On its exterior, close to the edge, are a dozen perforated projections. It is thought that these were used as handles when the mass was put into position. The summit is flat, and on it at one time a statue may have stood. Simplicity is almost always one of the characteristics of the great, and the mausoleum which he erected was worthy, in its strength and plainness, of Theodoric the Goth.

BOLOGNA

THE traveller in Italy must often have noticed the difference in the shape of the battlements that nowadays add so much to the picturesqueness of old towers and half-ruined fortress walls. No doubt he has heard the term "Guelph" or "Ghibelline" applied to them. It is supposed that "Welf" and "Waiblingen" were first used in Germany as battle-cries at the conflict of Weinsberg in 1140. When the struggle for the imperial throne between Philip of Swabia and Otto of Brunswick was hanging in the balance, the sympathies of Brescia, Milan, and other Lombard cities were enlisted on the side of Otto the Welf. In the subsequent feuds between the Pope's party and the Emperor's it became a necessity for the inhabitants of the cities of the northern part of the peninsula, if they wished to exist at all, to favour either one side or the other. The Guelph party were for the Pope, and the Ghibelline were partisans of the Emperor. And thus we find in the history of most of these towns an espousal, as policy dictated, of the Pope's cause at one time, and of the Emperor's some decades later. This apparent inconsistency was the outcome of family feuds within the city walls. For a term of years the Guelphic nobles might be in the ascendant, until, on the death or murder of a leading member, they succumbed to the prowess of the imperial party. The great families that pinned their faith to the ascendency of the latter adopted the swallow-tailed battlement on the towers of their castle walls, to distinguish them from the square-shaped that were already in existence. Italy throughout the middle ages was torn by internecine strife which was reflected throughout every class of society, and the subject of this chapter was no exception. Owning allegiance to the Pope, the Bolognese overran Romagna and forced the towns of that province to declare for the Church. In 1249 they defeated the Modenese at Fossalto and took King Enzio prisoner. For two-and-twenty years—in fact, for the rest of his life—they kept the unhappy man confined in the Palace of the Podestà, treated however, as we should treat a first-class misdemeanant, and according to his rank. The long-drawn-out feuds of the Lambertazzi and Gieremei families, and later on those between the great Visconti and Bentivoglio, kept the Bolognese in a perpetual state of faction fights, which lasted until the warlike Pontiff Julius II. annexed the city to the States of the Church.

To go back to its earliest days, we learn that the Etruscan king, Felsina, founded a city in 984 B.C. where Bologna now stands. He gave it his own name, and made it the chief of his twelve Etruscan cities. Bologna can thus, with legitimate pride, point to a history approaching three thousand years. We find it to-day a typical modern place, with just enough of the middle ages left to make it one of the most desirable of all North Italian cities. It possesses hardly a street which is not arcaded; and the thought arises: "How admirably adapted for street fighting were these sheltered walks in the days when one half of the town was at strife with the other!" In the oldest parts of the city the streets are tortuous and narrow. Arcades in such streets would be just the very best cover for raiders to steal along at night; and such must have been the terror of the inhabitants during centuries of discord that there is scarcely a house which has any windows opening into the arcades, and those that do are heavily barred. Walking through these streets, silent witnesses of bloody feuds and severe fights, one cannot suppress the feeling that the old quarters of Bologna are full of mystery, and it does not require much imagination to see the Visconti party creeping along in the shadowed ways for an attack on their hereditary foes, the Bentivoglio.

So much for the thoughts awakened by Bologna's narrow thoroughfares. Its chief open square is the Piazza Maggiore, as fine an old Italian square as can be found anywhere. The celebrated Fontana de Nettuno is in the centre. A nude bronze statue of the god by Giovanni da Bologna stands eight feet high, in a somewhat repellent attitude, above the pedestal and basin. It is always the centre of a lounging crowd which throngs the square throughout the day. On the west side of the Piazza is the Palazzo Pubblico, with a façade that still retains, despite restoration, traces of eight elegant pointed windows. A figure of the Virgin in terra-cotta, once gilded, stands under a good canopy high up on the empty space of the great wall of the façade. These comparatively empty wall spaces are a feature of Bolognese architecture of the thirteenth century. Pierced by a few windows, they give a great idea of solidity and strength; and though one finds the same character in the palaces of Tuscan cities, it is not so prominent there as in the big buildings of Bologna. An immense entrance gateway opens into a courtyard, and from this a very fine staircase by Bramante leads up to the interior. In a smaller court beyond is a very beautiful cistern by Terribilia. The Hall of Hercules, so called from the colossal statue by Alfonso Lombardo, vies with the Sala Farnese in splendour. Up to the year 1848 the palace was the residence of the Legate and the Senator. The lower portion is now the chief post office of the city.

On the north side of the Piazza is the Palazzo del Podestà. It is a building that was begun at the commencement of the thirteenth century, but not until the year 1485 was the façade erected. Of magnificent proportions, it is chiefly famous as the prison of King Enzio. The great saloon is still called the Sala del Re Enzio, and among other vicissitudes was at one time a theatre, and at another the court in which the national game of *pallone* was played. A solid-looking and lofty tower, the Torrazzo dell' Aringo, rises at one end of the façade above the arcades. On the piers which carry the arches of these may still be seen the huge wrought-iron brackets, the rings, and the sockets for supporting banner poles and holding lighted torches.

Along the east side of this part of the Piazza which is **L**-shaped, is the Portico de' Banchi, a continuous arcade, extending beyond the limits of the square the whole length of Bologna's great church. This, the church that the Bolognese in their pride intended should be the largest in Italy, has not been completed beyond the commencement of the transepts. The nave and aisles alone are finished; they are three hundred and eighty-four feet long, and the width, including the chapels, measures one hundred and fifty. The building is proportionately high, and, as will be seen in the illustration, is very spacious. It was commenced in 1390 and dedicated to S. Petronio. The architect, Antonio Vincenzi, was one of the celebrated *Riformati*, and went as ambassador to the Venetian Republic in 1396.

The Piazza Maggiore slopes downwards from the south. S. Petronio is situated at its southern end, and orientates south by west. The façade therefore faces north-east, and for the construction of a level floor the great church is placed at this end some dozen steps above the sloping Piazza. In the museum attached to S. Petronio there may be seen the original designs, elevations, and a model of the finished structure. Had funds permitted, this façade, placed so well, and with such magnificent buildings surrounding it, would have been one of the best Italian attempts to realise a Gothic church. As it is, it is a grand scheme unfulfilled.

The lower portion of the façade is extremely good, the three canopied doorways being pure Italian Gothic. They are adorned with bas-reliefs which represent different scriptural events from the Creation onwards. Tribolo, an intimate friend of Benvenuto Cellini, was responsible for the beautiful angels and sibyls round the arch of that on the left hand. The fine bas-relief of the Resurrection in the lunette, where Christ is seen among sleeping soldiers, is by Alfonso Lombardi. The central portal is considered the masterpiece of Jacopo della Quercia, who was not overpaid by the three thousand golden florins he received for the work, considering that it took him twelve years to complete. His noble figure of the Almighty, surrounded by thirty-two patriarchs and prophets, is extremely fine. The right-hand doorway is another example of Tribolo's purity of style. The brickwork of the exterior is covered, round the whole church at the base, by a very fine base-table of white marble with good mouldings. In the model the entire brick surface is hidden by the same material. The buttresses are good, and so are the pointed windows of the aisles, some of which, by the way, contain good glass.

The interior is very lofty and expansive. Twelve immense piers carry the arches of the nave, twenty-four smaller ones those of the aisles. The height of all these may be judged from the illustration, wherein also the peculiar

Italian Gothic capital is seen. Milan's great cathedral and S. Anastasia in Verona are other specimens of the same style of capital. They appear to be stuck on to the columns, of which they seem to form a part, rather than a separate cap for the arches to rest on. One hardly knows how this particular style grew or where it emanated, but it is not unlike the palm-leaf capital of an Egyptian column. The aisles are rather shallow for the width of the nave. The side chapels are shut off from them by good metal grilles or beautiful marble screens. Four very ancient black pillars with crosses engraved stand against four of the aisle piers. They are supposed to have been placed at the gates of old Bologna by S. Petronio himself, and are much venerated by the Bolognese. On the floor of the church is traced the celebrated meridian line of Gian Domenico Cassini. Under the immense canopy which stands over the high altar Charles V. was crowned in 1530 by Pope Clement VII. The Emperor had been invited to Italy by the last of the Ducal House of Sforza, and with his coronation commenced the foreign occupation of North Italy.

Bologna's cathedral is dedicated to S. Pietro. It is situated in the Via dell' Indipendenza, but is so wedged in between the high buildings which adjoin it on both sides that it is difficult to find. S. Pietro is a huge barn-like edifice commenced in the bad period of 1605. It is a very ancient foundation with no redeeming architectural features. The most interesting thing it contains is Ludovico Carracci's celebrated "Annunciation." After the scaffolding had been removed on the completion of the work which is over the arch above the high altar, Carracci discovered some bad drawing in one of the figures. He died soon after this—from grief, so the story goes, as the authorities would not permit him to re-erect it at his own cost and remedy the defect.

Figure 20: INTERIOR OF S. PETRONIO, BOLOGNA

INTERIOR OF S. PETRONIO, BOLOGNA

The church of S. Stefano, or rather the seven different edifices which are thus named, occupies the site of a temple of Isis. It stands below the level of the little Piazza de S. Stefano, and on its exterior wall is one of the open-air pulpits not uncommon in Italy. The first church, called Il Crocifisso, is of the sixteenth century and not interesting. From a door in the north wall one goes down half a dozen steps into the second church of the Santo Sepolcro. This is a circular building, supposed to have been the old baptistery. Twelve columns, brick and marble alternating, support a good Romanesque gallery under the dome. The six marble shafts came from the pagan temple. In the centre is a grand altar-pulpit, which has a stairway leading up on either side. Under the altar is an urn which at one time held the remains of S. Petronio. On the stone floor a shutter of iron covers the well that possesses miraculous properties, these having been imparted to it by the saint. The church dates from the tenth century. An iron grille in one of the walls shuts off the oldest church of all, a basilica of the fourth century. It is dedicated to SS. Paolo e Pietro. Forty-eight columns with Byzantine and Greek capitals support the brick barrel vault of the nave. This is dimly lighted by small round clerestory windows. The altar stands in the tribune at the top of much-worn limestone steps. This also has a brick vault. At the end of the narrow aisles are the sarcophagi of S. Agricola and S. Vitalis—Bologna's S. Vitalis. The next church, if it may be so called, is formed by the small court known as the Atrio di Pilato. It has never been touched since the eleventh century, and contains a very ancient font. Down more steps is the church of the Confessio. This old crypt must be a good twenty feet below the level outside. The quadripartite vaulting is borne by thick stunted columns that are barely five feet high, though one is said to be the exact height of Christ. It is very dark, and dates from the tenth century. The sixth church is the passage which leads to the seventh and last, that of the Trinity. Four rows of columns with Byzantine and Romanesque capitals support the roof of this square building. In one of the chapels, in a galleried niche, there is an extraordinary life-sized wooden group of the Adoration of the Magi. Mary wears a crown of brass studded with uncut stones. On the Child's head is a mitre of the same. The expressive faces of the Three Kings, who bring offerings, are extremely naïve. The first wears the conical hat of the ancient shepherds of the hills of Venetia that one still comes across in out-of-the-way districts.

The adjoining cloisters of the suppressed Celestine monastery are remarkable in the solidity of the short pillars, not four feet high, which form the lower colonnade. These are in absolute contradistinction to the elegant double shafts of the upper gallery. The brickwork throughout the whole of S. Stefano is very good. Concentric patterns, squares, chequer work where small squares of marble and glazed tiles have been introduced, diamonds, and oblongs are arranged in a perfect harmony of design the like of which one cannot find in Italy. The exterior of S. Sepolcro is, in this respect, unsurpassed.

Bologna's university is one of the oldest in Italy, and the first in which academical degrees were conferred. It was founded in 1119 by Irnerius. Numerous schools were established in the West after Byzantine authority had faded away. Among the first was that of Bologna, where Pepo began to expound the law in 1075. Irnerius followed him five-and-twenty years later and introduced the Justinian code. His followers became known as Glossatori, a word derived from the Greek   , originally meaning a *tongue*. The last of these glossators was Accursius, who compiled the *glossæ* known as the "Glossa ordinaria," a work which soon became the acknowledged authority. The visitor who wanders through the city and finds himself in the market-square will there see outside the church of S. Francesco three canopied tombs. The sarcophagi which rest on a platform borne by pillars are those of three Glossatori, and one of them contains the remains of Accursius. The canopies of these tombs are covered with green tiles. S. Francesco is a fine Gothic church with two elegant *campanili*. It is undergoing extensive restoration, and, though of some architectural interest, does not compare in other ways with that of S. Domenico.

This church, wherein repose the remains of the founder of the Order of Preaching Friars or Dominicans, was begun with the intention of following the prevailing fashion of the day and constructing another Gothic fabric. Except for the pointed windows in some of the chapels, S. Domenico bears no traces of this intention. The interior of white marble, in a medley of styles in which poor Renaissance predominates, is very cold. The exterior has a very heavy frieze of white marble; the commencement of its outer covering carried no further than this. It is seen in the sketch, which also shows the canopied tomb of the learned jurist, Rolandino Passageri, who was selected by the city to frame the reply to the letter in which the Emperor Frederick II. demanded the release of his illegitimate son Enzio. In the church lie Guido Reni, whose tomb is in the chapel shown with the heavy frieze, and his talented fellow-artist Elisabetta Sirani, King Enzio, Taddeo Pepoli, Captain of the People in 1334, and the great S. Dominick.

Figure 21: S. DOMENICO, BOLOGNA

S. DOMENICO, BOLOGNA

Born in Old Castile in 1170, S. Dominick was ordained priest in 1198. His fiery zeal against "heretics" and his extraordinary preaching powers soon brought him into great prominence. He was instrumental in establishing courts for trial and punishment of obstinate "heretics." The commissioners, who were invested with a jurisdiction that gave them powers of torture, and life and death, were known as "Inquisitors," and their conclaves paved the way for the dreaded Inquisition. S. Dominick's tomb is one of the finest in North Italy. It is one of the earliest works that the genius of Niccolò Pisano produced, having been completed thirty years before his masterpiece at Pisa was begun. A magnificent iron grille separates the chapel from the nave. On the top rail are four very charming little figures in bronze of saints. The tomb is adorned by bas-reliefs illustrating the chief events in the life of the saint. Below these is a very delicately carved set of smaller ones by Alfonso Lombardi, which form a sort of *predella*, and are nearly three hundred years later. The urn which contains the saint's remains is behind the upper set. A small statue of S. Petronio in front is by Michael Angelo, and the best of the beautiful little angels at the corners claims the same hand as its sculptor. Cherubs at the top of the monument hold two very heavy festoons of flowers, which somewhat mar the fine composition of the whole. From this it is evident that the exuberance of Pisano's youth had yet to learn the reticence which comes with age.

No description of Bologna would be complete without mention of its wonderful towers. The graceful Torre Asinelli rises to a height of three hundred and twenty-one feet, and, although nearly four feet out of the perpendicular, tapers upwards so imperceptibly that the inclination is not noticeable. Close by it stands the Torre Garisenda, built by the two brothers Garisenda. It leans ten feet in one direction and three in another, and rises to a height of one hundred and sixty feet. Although the guide-books tell one it was thus constructed, it has undoubtedly sunk into its position, as the different stages inside slope with the inclination of the tower. These two are not the only towers of Bologna, but, being situated in the centre of the oldest quarters of the city, are those that are best known.

PARMA

PARMA is very much like any other of the smaller cities of Italy. It can however boast of a prehistoric lake-dwelling settlement, unearthed in 1864, and a still later, though very early origin as an Etruscan colony. To-day it is a bright little place pleasantly situated on the broad stream that gave it its name. If it were not, however, for its cathedral, its ancient baptistery, and its inseparable connection with the art of Correggio, there would be but little to interest the stranger or even call for a halt at its railway station. Four bridges span the river Parma, and from each the blue line of the Apennines may be seen stretching away over the tops of the orchards until lost in the distant haze. The old Roman road, the Via Æmilia, which we have already seen started out of Rimini, bisects Parma from east to west, and crosses the river by a fine old bridge, the Ponte de Mezzo. This is the only structure of the four which can lay claim to any age. It has a narrow roadway inclining up to the centre with high parapets on either side, and partakes very much of the character of a Roman edifice. Except for a few inscribed slabs there is nothing of any consequence left to remind one that the pleasant little city of to-day was once a flourishing colony of Imperial Rome. In the Guelph and Ghibelline feuds it espoused the Pope's cause and successfully withstood a siege by Frederick II. In 1341 it came into the hands of the Visconti, Dukes of Milan, and was associated with that duchy for two hundred years. Pope Julius II. incorporated it with the Papal States, and thirty years after this the reigning Pope, Paul III., gave it to his natural son Pietro Luigi Farnese. This family supplied seven dukes to Parma where they reigned until the male line became extinct in the year 1731. The Bourbons came into possession of the duchy through Marie Louise, and with the assassination in the public thoroughfare of Duke Charles III., its history may be said to have come to an end.

The cathedral and baptistery, with the ecclesiastical buildings which form the square in which they stand, make a group of much interest. The first named is a very fine example of Romanesque work. It was commenced in 1058, but not consecrated until fifty years later, nor really completed till the middle of the thirteenth century. The façade is however entirely the original design.

Figure 22: THE CATHEDRAL AND BAPTISTERY, PARMA

THE CATHEDRAL AND BAPTISTERY, PARMA

Two rows of arcades traverse its length; the lower is on a level with and carried through the upper portion of the central porch. A third follows the line of the gable under a heavy cornice. The porch is similar to the one illustrated of Verona's cathedral. Two colossal lions bear the burden of the double canopies and were the work of Bono da Bisone. The sun is sculptured on the keystone of the arch, and in the soffits the months are illustrated by a series of reliefs of agricultural pursuits, as in S. Mark's at Venice. A good many Roman tablets have been used as decoration and for building material along the whole façade. Two other doors, as well as the central portal, give entrance to the church. The only other feature of the exterior worth mention is the beautiful red brick *campanile* with its green tiled spire.

The first impression one receives of the interior is that of extreme solemnity and great majesty. It never wears off. The high altar, a blaze of silver and gilt, stands well placed eighteen steps above the nave. The transepts also are thus situated, and there is enough length in the seven bays that separate the aisles from the nave to put the choir well back from the spectator as he enters at the west door. From the high altar the eye instinctively travels upwards to the spandrils in the drum of the dome where part of Correggio's grand frescoes are seen. The fourteen fluted columns of the nave are quadrangular. Seven have Corinthian capitals and seven are Romanesque with traces of Byzantine origin in the figures, beasts and birds which form the volutes. Some of these are peacocks with curling outstretched necks; others are the heads and upper limbs of human figures. The triforium gallery has elegant pillars in pairs, that support round arches. The clerestory is placed very high. The vaulting of the nave is peculiar, it is elliptical. The whole of the walls are covered with frescoes by Lattanzio Gambara and Girolamo Mazzuola, who was a pupil of Parmigianino. A frieze is above the capitals of the fluted pilasters that support the arch of the choir and runs on into the transepts. It is symbolical of the strength of the Church. Lions are seen here hunting antelopes, deer, and other animals; that is, the Church is chasing away all evil doers.

The crypt under the choir is architecturally interesting, as it shows in some of the capitals of its thirty-eight columns the evolution from pure Byzantine to Lombardo-Romanesque work. But perhaps it will be the frescoes in the dome that draw visitors to this fine church rather than its architectural features. In the decoration of this Correggio surpassed himself in his mastery of *chiaroscuro* and the foreshortening of the human figure. The "Assumption of the Virgin," though very adversely criticised when finished, and now greatly injured by damp and neglect, is still one of the grandest paintings of its sort extant.

Almost adjoining the south-west corner of the cathedral, and built on sloping ground, stands Parma's celebrated baptistery. It was begun in the year 1196, from designs by Benedetto Antelami. The construction was for many years very spasmodic, and wholly ceased when the bloodthirsty Ezzelino da Romana governed North Italy for Frederick II. in the thirteenth century, and forbade the inhabitants to quarry any more marble. At his death it was pushed on, and in the end finished towards the close of that century, a date which accounts for the pointed arches at the top of the interior. It is built of Verona marble, and is an octagon with three arched portals, on which are some very interesting sculptures of Old Testament history. Jacob, out of whom grows a tree in the branches of which are his brothers with Moses at the top, is on one side of the north door. Another tree, with David and Solomon and the Prophets, is a pendant on the other. The south doorway is decorated in a similar style, but the trees are full of all the birds apparently then known. Barn-door fowls, storks, parrots, eagles, ducks, and peacocks, &c. &c., find a place in this extraordinary aviary in stone. Signs of the Zodiac form a sort of frieze on the lower portions of the eight sides of the exterior. Four tiers of columns forming open galleries support a continuous architrave, which, whatever the architectural merits, is not artistically a pleasing arrangement. The interior is sixteen-sided. Between each division a long marble shaft is carried from its base on the floor right up to the converging ribs of the pointed vaulting. The whole of the walls and vault are covered with frescoes. The upper are early, and appear to be almost contemporaneous with the finishing of the building. The lower bear the names of Niccolo da Reggio and Bartolino da Piacenza, and are of fourteenth-century date. The Life of John the Baptist naturally takes precedence in these interesting examples of mural decoration. The huge font in the centre of the baptistery is cut out of a single block of marble. It has a centre compartment like that already described in S. Giovanni in Fonte, in Verona. The registers of the baptistery go back as far as the year 1459, since when it is known that all the babies born in Parma have been received into the Faith within its walls.

The church of S. Lodovico, also called S. Paolo, was formerly attached to a Benedictine nunnery. Correggio's celebrated series of pagan frescoes cover the walls of the "parlour" of the nunnery. They were executed to the order of the abbess, Giovanna da Piacenza, and are more fitted for a "Trianon" than a convent. Minerva, Juno, Bacchus, and other heathen gods and goddesses, with Cupids, and such-like profanities, are most charmingly arranged amidst a lattice pattern of flowers and foliage. At the period, the beginning of the sixteenth century, when this dainty scheme was painted, great licence and irregularities prevailed in some of these conventual establishments. The abbess and her nuns often entered into all the gaieties of the outside world and indulged in the vices pertaining to it. In this case the wrath of the austere Adrian VI. was visited on Giovanna and her flock, and S. Paolo was closed, the abbess dying within a month after this humiliation.

GENOA

THE poet Tasso in his "Jerusalem Delivered" sings of the exploits of the great commander of the First Crusade; and although Godfrey de Bouillon had little to do with Genoa, it was from its port that his fleet spread sail in 1096 and disappeared over the southern horizon on its way to the Holy Land. Nearly three years had passed in hard fighting before Godfrey and his army found themselves before the walls of Jerusalem. Meanwhile the Second Crusade had started from Genoa, under the command of Guglielmo Embrianco. He joined forces with De Bouillon, and the Holy City fell to their arms on July 15, 1099. Embrianco covered himself with glory; and on his return, among other treasures, brought home the celebrated Sacro Catino, which he presented to his native city. This dish of green glass is in the Cathedral. For centuries it was supposed to have been fashioned from a single emerald, and tradition has it as the very dish, the Holy Grail, which held the Paschal Lamb at the Last Supper.

The port of Genoa is very different now to what it was in those early days. Ships of all nationalities and every sort of build find refuge behind the numerous breakwaters which protect them from every gale that blows. The Molo Vecchio is the oldest of these shelters, and built upon half its length is an old quarter that is one of the fast-vanishing slums of the city. On the sea-ward side of this mole the Mura della Malapaga frowns on incoming craft, just as when in days gone by it bid defiance to the enemies of Genoa whose temerity had led them thus far in attacks on the city. It is terminated by a grand sea-gateway of very massive construction. At the end of a subsequent extension the old lighthouse rises, now well within the port. The house still stands in the old quarter in which Marco Polo was imprisoned after the defeat of the Pisans at the battle of Curzola, when he was taken captive. The Molo Nuovo stretches from the west side of the port near the tall Pharo, and, running outwards, bends back and covers the Molo Vecchio from the southerly gales.

Figure 23: AN OLD STREET, RAVENNA

AN OLD STREET, RAVENNA

Genoa's quays present a busy picture with the endless traffic that makes her the premier port of Italy. Strings of heavily laden carts drawn by teams of great mules are continually passing to and fro. Cabs rattle on the pavements, their drivers cracking their whips, the horses' heads decorated with the long tail feathers of the Amherst pheasant that dance about to the music of the harness-bells. Groups of boys play pitch and toss with coins, and still cry "Croce e Griffo" ("Cross or Gryphon"), a cry as old as the wars with Pisa. Itinerant pedlars pester folk to buy what no one seems to want. Under the arcades that face the sea-front shops of all sorts exhibit everything the seafarer can possibly require, and a lively business goes on in restuffing the emigrants' mattresses with dry sea-weed or hay. Up, behind all this, narrow streets wind through the old parts of the city and form an intricate maze wherein it is not difficult to miss one's way. Many of the houses here are seven, eight, or nine storeys high. All the day's washing—and every day is washing day—hangs out from the windows on long bamboos, or flutters from a cord stretched across the confined thoroughfares. Fowls, in their inquisitive endeavours to find food, try to satiate an appetite which is never satisfied. They are all scraggy. Dark courtyards at the bottom of these tall dwellings teem with screaming children and scolding women who are engaged at the fountain troughs with the washing. The ear-splitting cries of hawkers hasten one's footsteps down the steep descents, and one dodges out of their way only to lose oneself in vain attempts to leave the picturesque but squalid quarters of old Genoa.

However fascinating these slums may be—and they can hold their own from the painter's point of view with those in any other Mediterranean port— it must be acknowledged that the palaces for which Genoa is justly famous have hardly a rival. Historically the most interesting is the Palazzo di S. Giorgio, which stands close to the quayside at the east end of the Piazza Caricamento. It was erected in 1261 by Guglielmo Boccanegra, Captain of the People, for his own residence. At his death it was taken over as the government office for the registration of public loans, or *compere*, and named the Palazzo della Compere. In 1407 the Banking Company which practically ruled commercial Genoa acquired it as their headquarters, and its name was changed to that of the city's patron saint. This bank was the oldest in the world. It originated after the Genoese had driven the Venetians out of Constantinople, and so crippled the trade of their great Adriatic rival that for a time they were masters of nearly all the Eastern commerce that flowed westwards. This increase in prosperity was to a great extent the cause of the formation of a trading company, which accepted deposits and advanced loans to others than its own members. Thus was founded a bank that carried on its business successfully until the last Doge of Genoa was unseated and the mushroom Republic of Liguria proclaimed. The bank's property was then confiscated, and Genoa, governed by time-servers and place-hunters, fell upon evil days.

The Palazzo has been much altered and restored, but retains some of the original Genoese Gothic of Boccanegra's building. The Grand Hall on the first floor contains many statues of the city's benefactors and prominent men, and is an interesting epitome of their charities, which are commemorated on tablets attached to each. Some of these statues are seated, others are standing. The former are of men who purchased their niche in this Temple of Fame by payment of one hundred thousand livres to the state; while those who wished to be handed down to posterity at a cheaper rate had to content themselves with effigies that for ever are on two legs. The building is now the Customs House, and so once more money passes through different hands within its walls.

There are no other streets in Italy which can boast such an array of noble houses as the renamed Strada Nuova, now the Via Garibaldi, and the Via Balbi. The Palazzo Rosso has a magnificent *sala* that has a roof decorated with the armorial bearings of the Brignole family and those they intermarried with. The Municipality is now lodged in the Palazzo Doria Tursi. It has a grand façade flanked by open arcades with gardens on top, and was built for one of the Grimaldi by Rocco Lurago, a Como architect. Christopher Columbus was born in Genoa, and a bust of him stands in the great hall of the palace, the Sala della Giunta. In its pedestal are some of his autograph letters to the Banco di S. Giorgio. His family came from Piacenza, but at the time of his birth his father was warden of the Porto dell' Olivella, one of the city gates. The Palazzo Ducale, a huge building of mixed styles, was begun in the thirteenth century but not finished until the sixteenth. The Palazzo Durazzo has a grand vestibule and the finest staircase of all. The Palazzo Doria, standing alone in a delightful garden which extends towards the harbour, is beautified by a good *loggia* with arcades. Many are the palaces built by the great families of Genoa, the Spinola, Pallavicini, Balbi, Fieschi, Cambiasco, and others, as well as those already mentioned. They all contain large collections of pictures and other treasures, and it can certainly be said that the old nobility have left a hall-mark on their city. The earlier buildings all possessed towers, and during the Guelph and Ghibelline feuds, when street fighting was ever recurrent, these vantage positions were of immense strategic value—it was so pleasant to put the opposing faction *hors decombat* by pouring boiling pitch and molten lead on to the heads below! Street fighting became at length such a nuisance to the peaceable inhabitants that the order went forth that all towers were to be demolished, with one exception, the tower that Guglielmo Embrianco attached to his house. This alone was spared. And it is due to the veneration in which his name was held that it stands to-day the solitary defensive relic of Genoa's family feuds. It will be noticed that some of these palaces are faced, like the Cathedral, with bands of black and white marble. This distinction was granted to the four noble houses of Doria and Spinola, who were adherents of the Pope, and Fieschi and Grimaldi, who took the Emperor's side in all wars.

The Cathedral is a good example of what may be termed Genoese Gothic. It is dedicated to S. Lorenzo, and was consecrated by Pope Gelasius II. in 1118. The façade, separated into three unequal parts, is a good example of thirteenth-century Gothic. The *piazza* on to which it faces slopes sharply downhill—all Genoa is up and down hill—and the Cathedral rises well on its tier of steps. Bands of black and white form the exterior wall of the whole building, and are effectively carried through the recesses of the portals. The centre porch has twisted columns, which are carried round the splay of the arch. The columns themselves alternate with others that are circular. The bases and pedestals are covered either with carving or inlaid chequer and lozenge patterns. The two flanking porches are similar, and assist very greatly to increase the pleasing effect of this somewhat elaborate treatment, which is heightened by the two detached spiral columns on either side and those that terminate the façade at each end. In the tympanum over the central doorway is a figure of S. Lawrence lying nude on a gridiron. The fire beneath is stoked and kept alive by bellows handled by those who assisted at his martyrdom.

Above is a figure of the Almighty surrounded by an angel, a lion, a peacock, and a deer. The detached column at the south-west angle of the façade, seen in the illustration, carries a figure of the patron saint under a canopy. It rests on the back of a lion; four smaller beasts of the same species encircle the base. The two huge *couchant* lions at either end of the steps are of much later date than these. From the south-west angle a fine turreted tower rises upwards from the square, and with its copper dome forms a great feature of the Cathedral as one walks up the Strada Carlo Felice. This street is narrow and full of traffic, so much so that it is with difficulty one makes out the many mutilated tablets with Roman inscriptions, built haphazard into the south wall of the Cathedral, and the canopied mediæval tombs let in above.

Figure 24: FAÇADE OF THE CATHEDRAL, GENOA

FAÇADE OF THE CATHEDRAL, GENOA

The interior of the building is disappointing. One expects to find more space. A gallery at the west end, under which you find yourself directly upon entering, forms a sort of atrium. It is supported by very massive clustered columns which carry a good groined vault with heavy ribs. This was originally the *cantoria*, or organ-loft. Nine small bays on either side separate the nave from the aisles. The single columns of the arches are of red and purple marble from the renowned quarries at Tortosa, in Spain. At each corner of the black marble bases, and touching the *torus* of the column, the head of a bird or animal has been carved. The arches of the bays are pointed. Above them is an open triforium formed by rows of small stunted arches that are carried by single and clustered columns in banded black and white. The clerestory is of small narrow single lights. The transepts are Renaissance, and the choir a mixture of styles.

The chapel of St. John the Baptist in the north aisle bears a resemblance to that of "Il Santo" at Padua. Four slender carved pillars support the entablature of good Renaissance design, on which are exceptionally well arranged panels illustrating the saint's life. Filippo Doria erected the canopy borne by porphyry columns which stands over the altar. Under this, enclosed in an iron casket within a marble ark, on which are sculptured reliefs, are the remains of St. John.

Genoa's fleet was homeward bound after one of the crusades, when, through stress of weather, it took shelter in the port of Myrra, in Lycia. Hearing that a monastery close by contained the sacred remains of the saint, some of the bolder spirits of the fleet entered the church attached, and, despite the protests of their co-religionists, carried off in triumph all that remained of St. John. The relics were presented to their own Cathedral of S. Lorenzo on arriving home. Here they have rested ever since. No women are admitted into the chapel—a prohibition imposed by Pope Innocent VIII. in remembrance of the guilt of Herodias. The Treasury holds many things of value and interest besides the Sacro Catino already described. Among them is a fine piece of Byzantine much-bejewelled metal work known as the Cross of Zaccaria. It was carried off from Phocea by Ticino Zaccaria at the capture of that place.

The church of S. Bartolommeo degli Armeni contains the celebrated picture on a cloth of the head of Christ. It was given to one of the Montaldi, a noble Genoese family, by John Paleologus, Emperor of Constantinople, in return for important services rendered. The legend runs that Agbarus, King of Edessa, sent an artist, Annanias by name, to paint our Lord's portrait. Annanias was no portrait painter, and failed in the attempt. Our Lord then took a cloth, pressed it to His face, and sent the impression back to the King. Leonardo Montaldo bequeathed it to the church in 1382.

The church of S. Donato, with its Romanesque tower that was built into the walls of Genoa forming one of its defences, dates from the eleventh century. There are many other ecclesiastical fabrics in a place which is fast losing all traces of old associations. Of the three sets of walls built at different times as the city slowly enlarged itself, the outer alone bears any semblance of its pristine state, and modern Genoa, with up-to-date improvements, is encroaching on these. But for all this its situation is superb, and it is in every way a bright and charming place. To those who enter by rail it is impossible to grasp the incomparable position the city occupies. Coming in along the Cornice road from the west, or that from the east, it can be better realised. But the best approach is by sea. The long line of distant mountains that first appears on the horizon gradually opens up, peak rises beyond peak, the nearer hills become detached, valleys are revealed, and soon white houses may be discerned dotting the dark grey slopes. A long, broken array of villages fringes the blue waters, gathering closer together as land is approached. The mass of warm yellowish tint scintillating in the brilliancy of a Mediterranean sun takes shape, and the eye by degrees separates long terraced rows of buildings, church towers and domes from one another. The colour changes, and a heterogeneous combination of pink, white, yellow, and grey discloses the far-famed city rising tier above tier from the busy port that lies at its base. A whistle sounds, the rattling cable rushes out, the anchor plunges into the water, and our ship is at rest. We are in the historic port from which the First Crusade started, and from which not so long ago the patriot Garibaldi, with the friendly aid of Rubattino, sailed with his devoted thousand for Sicily.

PISA

YOU will not find in all Italy anything that is placed quite so well with an eye to effective grouping as the Baptistery, Cathedral, and Campanile of Pisa. Nowhere does anything approach so near to the ecclesiastical exclusiveness of an English cathedral close as the great square of level green sward in which these three remarkable fabrics stand. From one corner of the Piazza del Duomo part of the university buildings looks over the turf to the Baptistery. Hard by the seat of learning is the Porta Nuova, a fine gateway that pierces the old walls of the city—walls of an almost unpaintable red. Within the walls, on the other side of the Cathedral—that is, to the north—the Campo Santo stands with bare façade and domed tower. Adjoining it on the east, conventual buildings and the Palace of the Archbishop occupy the angle of the Piazza. They face the Campanile. The one or two establishments which come next as we continue our *giro* are full of little marble "Leaning Towers" and other souvenirs which the tourist delights in. Save for the intrusiveness of these shops, there is nothing else in the surroundings of the vast square that detracts from the fascination of the wonderful group in the centre.

The Pisa of to-day cannot have changed much from the Pisa of two hundred years ago. It is true that, outside the old walls which encircle her, a straggling suburb is growing up, but within them noble palaces still front the River Arno, and others occupy the best positions in the city. Dwellings of the poorer classes line the narrow streets that connect the wider and more spacious thoroughfares; they crowd thickly together, and the life of the pavements is the life of Italy as the tourist loves to find it—the life of days gone by.

It has been said that all roads lead to Rome; in Pisa all roads lead to the Piazza del Duomo. In the centre stands the Cathedral; to the west of it, the Baptistery; to the east rises the Campanile, or Leaning Tower. Pisa had well-nigh reached the zenith of her power when in 1063 her people resolved to commemorate a great victory over the Saracens by building a new cathedral. Ninety years later, having destroyed their Southern rival Amalfi, the Pisans commenced the Baptistery. The year 1174 saw the first stone of the Campanile laid. Thus in a little over one hundred years these three buildings, which mark so important an epoch in Italian ecclesiastical architecture, were under construction. The advent of a man of unknown origin, Busketus, who

93

designed the Cathedral, and whose epitaph is on one of its walls, heralded a new phase in the art of the country. And although he adapted something from the Romanesque, this grand church of his was the precursor of a style that we find amplified, but not improved upon, in Ferrara, Pavia, Parma, and, most notably of all, in the neighbouring city of Lucca. In the history of Italian ecclesiastical architecture Pisa stands pre-eminent.

The façade of the Cathedral is very striking. The seven round arches of the blind arcade that form the lowest tier or base are continued round the entire fabric. The pedestals from which the columns of this arcade spring rest on a bold but simple base-table that also encircles the building. These columns are round on the façade, the eastern apse, and the apse at the end of each transept, but become pilasters elsewhere. This extremely good arrangement does not break up the flat walls by too many obtrusive perpendicular lines. On the contrary, it enhances their noble length, and at the same time improves the semicircle of the apses. Three bronze doors occupy three arches of the façade arcade. They are good examples of the seventeenth century. Crude mosaics in the tympanums above are a jarring colour note which one would willingly suppress. It is otherwise, however, with the wonderful patterns of inlaid marble and the rich ornamentation of vine-leaves and floral forms, human heads and animals, that embellish the whole façade—a character of decoration that finds a fitting terminal in the crockets on the gables and the figures at their ends. Above the arcade four deeply recessed galleries fill the whole space of the façade. The lowest of these is on a level with the clerestory lights in the aisles. The next is cut off at either end by the angle of the gable; the columns diminish in size with the slope of the aisle roof. The third is in a line with the clerestory of the nave, and the topmost diminishes with the gable, which is carried beyond and above the ridge of the roof of the nave. The slender pillars that support the arches of these galleries have wonderfully carved capitals, and stand out in the brilliant afternoon sun from the deep shadow behind with marvellous effect.

One enters the Cathedral by the south and only door which escaped the great conflagration of 1596. Its bronze panels are by Bonannus, who has handed down twenty-four episodes of Gospel history in the very ingenuous style of his time. A lead-covered penthouse wards off the inclemency of the weather. The fine cupola which rises above the crossing is rather dwarfed by the Gothic arcade and finials which surround its base. The grand effect of the Cathedral is due in a measure to the mellowing of the white marble, which the sun has seemingly baked to a beautiful warm yellow and light red. On the north side, which is exposed to the bitter *tramontana* wind from the Monti Pisani, the marble is blistered and scored, and has acquired an ashen white that in this sunny land is not pleasant.

The interior is lofty. The effect obtained by the bands of black and white marble of which the walls are composed is not so embarrassing to the eye as in Siena's holy fane. The nave is divided into ten bays; the columns that support the round arches are magnificent monoliths of granite. These bays are carried in a continuous colonnade across the transepts and along their east and west walls. The aisles are double. As a consequence the forest of columns and arches is almost bewildering; and if it were not for the fine proportions of the nave, the eye would have but little rest from a multiplicity of shadows and disturbing spots of light. The pointed triforium, that is borne by the arches of the nave, is continued across the transepts into the choir. The base of the cupola at the crossing is elliptical, the length being east and west and the narrow sides north and south. The interior of the dome is covered with frescoes. The design of the six altars in each aisle is attributed to Michael Angelo. The transepts are terminated by two apsidal chapels with mosaics in the semi-domes said to be designed by Cimabue. The same origin can be more justly claimed by that which decorates the vault of the choir apse, and in which the great artist has depicted our Lord in Glory, and S. John. The pavements of the choir and crossing are exceptionally fine *opus Alexandrinum*. The huge bronze lamp that hangs, swinging slightly, from the coffered and gilded roof of the nave is supposed to have suggested to Galileo the idea of the principle of the pendulum.

To the west of the Cathedral is Pisa's beautiful Baptistery. This building was commenced by Diotisalvi in 1153, and continued later on in 1278. The lowest storey is of the first mentioned date, and, like the Cathedral, is composed of a blind arcade, pierced in this case with small round-headed windows. An open gallery circulates round the whole edifice above this. Its columns support round arches that are surmounted in piers by crocketed gables, pierced and cusped. A figure stands on the apex of each, while between every pair small open turrets thrust their pinnacles upwards. Above this gallery a series of windows with a similar arrangement breaks the base-line of the somewhat ugly pear-shaped dome. As a prevention against the corroding influence of the salt sea winds, this dome is tiled on its south-west surface. The other portion is covered with lead.

Figure 25: THE BAPTISTERY, PISA

THE BAPTISTERY, PISA

In the centre of the interior, generally entered by the door opposite the west façade of the Cathedral, stands the font in which baby Pisans have for many generations been baptized. Like others, it is made for total immersion. The walls which surround the appropriately "waved" black-and-white pattern of its floor are extremely beautiful. A delicately carved framework of marble encloses wonderful panels of inlaid mosaic somewhat in the style of the pulpit in the illustration to "Salerno." Six small basins are let into the walls of the font and are used now for the Holy Rite. Near the altar stands Niccolò Pisano's masterpiece. This hexagonal pulpit rests on seven slender columns of marble and granite. Some of these columns rise from their bases on the backs of lions, gryphons, and crouching human figures, thus in a way representing the dominion of the Word of God over creation. The rectangular panels of the pulpit stage are beautifully carved in high relief. Niccolò Pisano's art, which bears evident traces of pagan influence, is seen at its best in these panels of the Nativity, Adoration of the Magi, Presentation in the Temple, the Crucifixion, and Last Judgment. On the steps is a red marble pillar standing on the back of a lion. It supports a small marble book-rest from which the Epistle was read. The desk on the pulpit itself is placed on an eagle, and was used for the reading of the Gospel. Eight marble piers and eight granite columns support the gallery beneath the dome. The whole of this noble interior is very light and airy, and Pisan mothers should have more cause to hope for a bright future for their babes than their sisters in Parma, if a comparison is permissible between the bright cheeriness of the one place and the mystical gloom of the other.

The Campanile stands to the east of the Cathedral. Its base is some feet below the restful green of the grass that covers the whole of the Piazza. Four different architects carried out its erection during a period that extended over nearly two hundred years. The base, another blind arcade, was begun in 1174 by Bonannus; the fourth gallery was added by Benenato, the next two by William of Innsbrück, and the topmost by Tommaso. The foundations were unfortunately laid in sea-sand, and the tower settled at an angle that causes it to lean towards the south thirteen feet out of the perpendicular. Galileo utilised this feature for experiments on the velocity of falling bodies.

Figure 26: THE CAMPANILE AND DUOMO, PISA

THE CAMPANILE AND DUOMO, PISA

The Campo Santo, the dome of which is seen in the illustration to the right of the Cathedral, is a quiet cloistered court on the walls of which are an extraordinary series of frescoes. Those on the north wall, by the Florentine, Benozzo Gozzoli, who was a pupil of Fra Angelico, are the most interesting. The Gothic arches and slender columns of the cloister, and the well-kept garden-plot in the centre, out of which tall cypress-trees rear themselves in ordered array, add much to the dignity of this quiet spot.

The old Dominican basilica of Sta Caterina stands in a corner of the piazza of the same name. Great plane-trees almost hide from view its beautiful façade, which, like that of the Cathedral, is gabled and arranged in galleries. Here, however, these are Gothic, with trefoil cusped arches, developing in the topmost to cinquefoil, and giving an air of elegance to the whole that is lacking in the Cathedral. A comparison of the two façades ends with the opinion that while in Sta Caterina there is more grace, the Cathedral possesses more architectural fitness for the design and proportions of the outline. Diotisalvi built the little octagonal church of S. Sepolcro for the Knights Templars, and Niccolò Pisano erected the fine *campanile* attached to the church of S. Francesco. This tower is partly supported by consoles, or brackets, within the church. The staircase runs up both inside and outside its walls.

S. Stefano, which contains a S. George by Donatello, is close to the Carovana in the Piazza dei Cavalieri. The piazza is thought to be the old Roman forum. The Carovana was the Palace of the Knights of S. Stephen, and was another of Niccolò Pisano's works, and, although altered later on by Vasari, is a fine example of Domestic architecture. A double flight of steps leads up to the entrance-door, on either side of which are tall windows. The façade is covered with frescoes and adorned by six busts in niches of the first half-dozen Grand Dukes, Masters of the Order. The roof projects far out, and the eaves, supported by well-carved cantilevers, throw a deep shadow down the front of the palace. The Order of S. Stefano was founded in 1561 by Cosimo I., but never distinguished itself amidst the Orders of Chivalry, and was dissolved in 1869. A statue of the founder stands over a fountain in front of the steps.

Among the buildings that face the Arno, the Palazzo Lanfreducci, with the words "alla Giornata" and a chain pendant over the doorway, the Palazzo Lanfranchi, where Byron lived, and the fine old fortress-tower, the Torre Guelfa, are the most notable in a city that at one time disputed with the mighty Genoa the rule of the Mediterranean. The rivalry between these two maritime powers ended only when, after the disastrous battle of Meloria, the Genoese filled up the harbour of Pisa, and she became no longer of any account as a naval base.

LUCCA

LUCCA is one of the most delightful little cities in the peninsula, and its seventy-two churches, taken as a whole, the most interesting in Italy. In matters ecclesiastical it is one of the oldest foundations in the country, and is reputed to have been the first place to have embraced Christianity. The first bishop of Lucca, a disciple of S. Peter, was S. Paulinus, and the long line of prelates who followed him were elevated to the higher dignity of Archbishop in 1726. The canons of Lucca are mitred, and the prelate has the privilege of wearing the insignia of a cardinal. It was always a Ghibelline city; even in the days of the Countess Matilda its inhabitants sided with the imperial party. When the attempt of Francesco Burlammachi to confederate the Tuscan cities failed, the Luchesi formulated the *Martiniana* Law, which permitted only a few of the leading families to participate in the government. The result of this was a peace that prevailed for many years. But perhaps the most important historical event that occurred within its walls took place in far earlier days than the sixteenth century. The first triumvirate was formed when Julius Cæsar, Pompey, and the wealthy Crassus met and entered into an agreement whereby the power was divided between the three. More tangible relics of Roman occupation are to be found where the amphitheatre once stood. The oval form of this is well preserved in the extremely picturesque Piazza Mercato—the Market Place. The wooden stalls of the market folk are practically little huts with tiled roofs, that follow the lines of the amphitheatre seats in gracefully curved alleys. In the Pinacoteca may be seen a print dated 1785, in which the space is enclosed by a high wall. In the centre is a tastefully laid out garden adorned with statues and rose bushes, around which a horse race is in progress. Many columns used in the erection of churches, and fragments of all sorts built into the walls, are evidences of Lucca's importance among the colonies of ancient Rome.

Figure 27: THE PORCH OF THE CATHEDRAL, LUCCA

THE PORCH OF THE CATHEDRAL, LUCCA

The cathedral was founded as early as 573 by S. Frediano. The first building was close to the present Duomo, and was erected on the site of the church of S. Giovanni—a very interesting Lombard edifice. The square baptistery attached to S. Giovanni, with its original waved black and white pavement and ancient square font, is well worthy of study. Pope Alexander II., who supplied William of Normandy with a holy banner to assist in the invasion of England, consecrated the cathedral, which, although much altered in the fourteenth century, still bears the impress of the architectural vogue of the tenth. The façade was added in 1204 by Giudetto. A portico of three unequal arches supports three tiers of small arches. These form galleries diminishing in length as they rise one above the other to the horizontal cornice at the top. A magnificent square *campanile* rises at the south end of the portico. Huge iron braziers stick out under its battlements at the four corners. It seems to crush the arch that springs from one side of its base, out of all proportion with the other two. This is very apparent from a distance, and produces an uncomfortable feeling. But, when one makes the intimate acquaintance of the portico and begins to examine the exquisitely designed arabesques, &c., that decorate its arches, there is nothing but admiration for a mind that could play with stone as Giudetto has done in this case. The piers which support the three round arches have each four slender columns. These are beautifully carved with all manner of intricate patterns. On the central pier Eve is seen tempting Adam to eat of the Forbidden Fruit. They are at the base of a tree, which growing upwards spreads out branches whereon rest the early Kings of Israel and the Prophets. The exterior members of the arches are covered with finely cut foliage. The capitals are formed by the semi-Gothic classical acanthus leaves of the period. Above the *abaci* of the capitals three lions, crouching on consoles or brackets, grip in their thin claws a snake, a dragon, and a demon. Between two of the arches there is a good stone group of S. Martin dividing his coat with a beggar by the use of a bronze sword. The interior wall of the portico has a flat arcade of red marble columns and arches. Three doors give entrance into the cathedral. Their tympanums are decorated by well-executed reliefs. A double frieze runs along the wall. On the lower portion figures, engaged in agricultural pursuits, and the Signs of the Zodiac are cut; on the upper, the life of S. Martin depicted in a series of panels. Some excellent examples of *graffiti* work decorate part of the wall. The galleries of the façade are like those that appear in the illustration of the church of S. Michele.

The chief feature of the interior of the Duomo is a fine Gothic triforium. As in Pisa's Cathedral, this goes round the whole nave, transepts, which it also crosses, and choir, stopping short only at the apse. It is formed of double divisions of three pointed and cusped arches, which on the west wall are increased to groups of four each. The transepts are double. A massive pier in each carries the triforium across in a most effective manner. The nine bays on either side of the nave have round arches. The fine roof, which is vaulted and groined, is unfortunately spoilt by a very *bizarre* scheme of colour that is not redeemed by the beautiful glass in the windows of the apse. Half up the north aisle is an octagonal chapel built of marble, but almost entirely covered with gilt. It is known as the Tempieto, and contains the venerated relic of the Vólto Santo, or Holy Face. It is supposed to be an image of Our Lord, executed by Nicodemus, but is evidently a work of the eleventh century carved in two different species of wood. A much finer work of art is the beautiful tomb of Ilaria Caretti in the north transept. With her little dog, emblem of fidelity, at her feet, the figure of this gracious lady lies extended on a noble sarcophagus. Little winged *putti* surround its base, and it ranks among the best productions of the accomplished Jacopo della Quercia.

One of the most perfect Gothic arcades in all Italy is to be found in the church of Sta Maria della Rosa. It is situated close to the Archbishop's palace at the east end of the cathedral. The spaces between the pointed arches and the top lights of the church are filled with exquisitely carved cherubs peeping out from a mass of foliage. In the Piazza dei Servi stands another small church, that possesses a carved wooden roof not in any way inferior to the marvellous one that adorns the Badia in Florence. It was erected during the days when Lucca was a republic, and one panel has the coat of arms of the city, with two great leopards as supporters and "Libertas" for a legend.

The church of S. Frediano is close to the city walls. Its fine tower is seen on the right in the illustration. Frediano, or "Fair Hair," was a son of a King of Ulster. Trained in Galloway, he travelled to Rome, where he was well received by Pelagius I., and housed in the Lateran. He became Bishop of Lucca in 565, and after the destruction of the first cathedral by the Lombards commenced the erection of the present archi-episcopal edifice. The church is full of interest, and contains the huge rectangular block of stone, computed to weigh three tons, which the saint lifted into a cart drawn by oxen, and which was to be used in the building of his cathedral. There is a fine circular font in the church, with the Passage of the Red Sea carved on its panels by the unknown Magister Robertus. Close to this, in the chapel dedicated to the patroness of domestic servants, Sta Zita, is a good example of Giovanni Della Robbia's work. Most of the church is built from the stones of the Roman Amphitheatre. The altar is placed at the west end. The façade is a very dignified composition, in which an Ionic colonnade and a good mosaic of our Lord in glory play an important part. The grand *campanile*, however, is its glory. This rises with tiers of open arches; but here they depart from the usual plan and increase in pairs. One tier of a single pair is the lowest; above are two of three arches, and the next two of four arches. Two sides of this splendid tower are of greater width than the others.

Figure 28: LUCCA FROM THE CITY WALLS

LUCCA FROM THE CITY WALLS

In the sketch a distant tower can be seen on which is growing a clump of trees. It is attached to the beautiful, red-brick Palazzo Borghi, one of the two fine palaces in Lucca built in the Venetian Gothic style. The story goes that the tower was built by Paolo Guigni, and that on its top he planted trees, under which he gave a series of banquets to show his indifference for the enemy who were then besieging the city. A very pleasant walk leads us along under the grand limes and elm trees that compose the shady boulevards on Lucca's old walls. Many a good study of roofs and distant mountains, in which the bare crags and rugged peaks of the Carrara range form a fine background, can be obtained from these walls; and many a beautiful peep through the foliage on to gardens below will reward the painter who strays out of the accepted route and makes a sojourn in the bright little city.

The church of S. Michele has the most striking façade of any so-called Pisan-Gothic building. It is another work of Giudetto's, but is anterior to that which he added to the cathedral. It is interesting to note how the fine colonnade at the base of S. Michele's façade was amplified in the later work of the cathedral by the portico which takes its place. Between the columns of this colonnade the closed lozenge-shaped lights, a familiar feature in the churches of the Pisan style, give a certain amount of solidity by their deep shadows. Above is an open gallery, under which is a marvellously intricate frieze of arabesques. Some of the pillars of this gallery are covered with inlaid marble, others are twisted or decorated with chevrons. On two of them repulsive-looking dragons, snakes, and demons crawl downwards in high relief. At each end is a cluster of four slender columns bound by knots. The capitals are boldly cut, with heavy square *abaci*, from which bosses and floral work protrude. The corbels of the round-headed arches are composed of heads of animals and demons, and the arches themselves are beautifully inlaid with geometrical designs. The frieze above is divided into panels of *graffiti*, wherein lions, goats and birds, &c., are depicted in all sorts of attitudes. The gallery above this is very similar, but with even better pillars supporting its arches. It slopes upwards from the gable ends. Then comes the strange and airy feature of this remarkable façade—a false gable with two galleries ending in a pointed apex. Standing on canopied turrets at each end of the gable are angels blowing bronze horns. Their robes are embroidered with inlaid marble and their outspread wings are of bronze. On the *acroteria*, or pedestal, at the top, is a colossal statue of S. Michael with vestments adorned by a gilded pattern. His wings are formed of separate bronze plates to diminish wind pressure, and make a good note of colour against a blue sky. At the back of this false gable a flight of steps ascends from the roof to the statue. As will be seen in the illustration, the colonnade is carried along the other walls of the church and *campanile*. This again is a grand tower and like that of S. Frediano has two sides greater than the others. The interior of S. Michele is very simple, very beautiful and dignified, and quite unspoilt by any whitewash or colour.

Figure 29: S. MICHELE, LUCCA

S. MICHELE, LUCCA

There are many other churches worthy of description if space allowed, but passing mention must be made of the earliest known work of Niccolò Pisano. This is a relief of the "Deposition from the Cross" in the tympanum of the arch of a side door at S. Martino. There is much else to see in the compact and well-ordered little city that is situated so beautifully in a great bowl with mountains on every side. Much, too, to wonder at in the legend S.P.Q.L. that the *municipio* still writes up on public notices as a reminder of the days when its inhabitants made the laws that governed the Republic of Lucca.

FLORENCE

ALTHOUGH Florence has no doubt an Etruscan origin, her first historical record dates from the time of Tiberius. During his reign the inhabitants presented a petition to the august presence praying him to prevent the diversion of the River Clanis into the Arno. Through many subsequent vicissitudes she rose from an obscure beginning to be the centre of the Art of the civilised world. This was accomplished in the days when Florentines were not ashamed of "soiling the fingers with trade," and was due to the good taste and patronage of her wealthy merchant citizens, who took the keenest interest in the development of their city as the home of all things cultured. The Florence of to-day is rapidly becoming as cosmopolitan as London, and as a consequence has a growing trade in the manufacture of "antiques." But so great is the charm of this wonderful city that every year sees an addition to the long list of those, who coming from other lands, either rent a flat within the walls or occupy a villa outside. It is a charm that never dies—indeed, becomes intensified. Bitter winds may whistle through the draughty streets, and tearing down the Arno from the mountains howl across its bridges; the end of the "merrie" month may still see deep snow on the hilltops, yet no one who has once been in Florence, even under these undesirable conditions, but wishes to come again. And this charm—what is it? Is it that the city stands in the midst of a garden, a veritable bed of roses? Does it lie in her classic river along the banks of which Dante oftentimes wandered? Is it because Cimabue, Giotto, Leonardo, Michael Angelo, Raphael, the della Robbias, Fra Angelico, and Donatello, all were at their zenith in Florence? Go to the Pitti and Uffizi and marvel at their powers. Is it in her glorious buildings, her magnificent palaces, and the traditions of her great families—the Medici, Buondelmonti, Uberti? In all of these surely lies a charm that nothing can dissipate! Yes, in all these; but still there is a something beyond them, a subtle, indefinable spell that enwraps the senses and captures one body and soul in this Queen of cities.

Figure 30: OR S. MICHELE AND THE PALAZZO DELL' ARTE DI LANA,
FLORENCE

OR S. MICHELE AND THE PALAZZO DELL' ARTE DI LANA, FLORENCE

Of all the great Florentine trade-guilds, the Wool-weavers were the richest,
and the illustration shows a restored corner of their Hall with the redecorated
altar behind the iron grille. On the opposite side is the Gothic church of
Or S. Michele. Originally the site was occupied by a corn market, in the
loggia of which stood the figure of a much-worshipped Madonna. Walls were
built round the *loggia* and the market removed to the storey above. The
niches on the exterior of the church contain statues of the patron saints of
the numerous trade-guilds. Among them was a fine S. George, the patron
saint of the Armourers Guild, by Donatello. This is now in the Bargello,
having been replaced by a cast. The figures of SS. Mark and Peter were
gifts from the linen merchants and the butchers, and are by the same master-
hand. The best stained glass in Florence decorates the fine Gothic windows
of the church. Their very elaborate tracery is cleverly designed to get the

greatest effect from the top light—so necessary in the narrow and dark street. The *Misericordia* Brethren may be seen in the sketch carrying out one of the self-imposed tasks for which they receive no payment whatever. The Compagnia della Misericordia was founded by Pier di Luca Borsi in the year 1240. Men of all grades of society belong to the Order, and once a year attend a service in the cathedral, when they take a pledge to abstain from profane language. They nurse the sick, carry patients to the hospitals, and the dead to their last home. Every one who knows Florence is familiar with the hurrying footsteps of the black-robed figures as they proceed on their errands of mercy. The headquarters of this noble self-sacrificing Order are on the left in the illustration of the Campanile.

Those who recollect Florence in the eighties will remember that the picturesque old quarter, the Mercato Vecchio, occupied the site of the fine Piazza Vittorio Emmanuele. This pestilential plague spot, into which it was hardly safe to venture, was done away with in the years 1890-95. When the work of demolition was begun it was found to be so foul and insanitary that no house-breakers were allowed to touch a single stone until three months of stringent disinfection had elapsed. This is one of the very few clearances that have taken place in the heart of the city since the fifteenth century, and the thought of it carries one back to the days when that great reformer, Fra Girolamo Savonarola, set Florence on fire with his fierce disputations. A great bronze disc with a medallion portrait of the ascetic monk marks the spot in the Piazza della Signoria where he ended his days at the stake with two brave companions. In his little cell in the monastery of S. Marco there are two pictures which present us with the details of the tragedy. Save for the flight of steps that has taken the place of the platform where his judges are seen sitting, the Palazzo Vecchio, wherein he was condemned, is the same to-day as it was then. It is the grandest secular building in Florence, and this is saying a great deal. Built of huge blocks of rough stone, it was commenced in 1299 by Arnolfo di Cambio, and is a testimony to the splendid construction of the fourteenth century. The top storey projects on brackets from the walls, which stand four-square. Under these brackets are the Ghibelline and Guelph arms; the former is a white lily on a red ground, the latter a red lily on a white ground, quartered with the crescent of Fiesole. The present arms of Florence, so familiar all over the city, are a red fleur-de-lys with two sprays on a white ground. The battlements that surmount this storey are square-shaped Guelph, while those of the great tower which dominates this part of the city are the swallow-tailed Ghibelline. This fine landmark is three hundred and seven feet high, and has a projecting gallery underneath the *loggia* with which it terminates. The palace was built to accommodate the eight Priori, who, under the presidency of the Gonfaloniere, ruled Florence. It remained the seat of government for over three hundred years until Cosimo de Medici, having usurped the power, removed his court to the Pitti Palace.

From Michelozzo's beautiful *cortile*, which one enters first, a noble staircase ascends to the Salone dei Cinquecento. It was in this magnificent hall, where a statue of Savonarola is now placed, that he was tried and condemned. There are other fine rooms in the Palazzo Vecchio, but nothing approaches the beauty of the little *cortile* below. Nine columns of grand proportions bearing round arches support the arcade that forms part of the courtyard. Each column has a different design above the fluting which runs half-way up them all. The delicate low relief of these exquisitely modelled devices, some of which are grape clusters, others children with garlands, heads, and classic ornamentation, is so slight, that the effect on every column obtained by the light which pours down from high above makes each one seem a simple mass of half-tone thrown strongly out against the deep shade of the arcade beyond. It is an architectural masterpiece of what the painter calls "values." A delightful fountain in the centre of the *cortile*, by Verrochio, adds to the sense of repose that one experiences when the glare and noise of the piazza are left behind.

The south side of the Piazza dei Signoria is taken up by the Loggia dei Lanzi—a good specimen of the domestic Gothic style of Italy. Three arches form the base that supports the lower storey. A rich balustrade and projecting cornice adorn the top. Benvenuto Cellini's "Perseus," and "Judith and Holofernes" by Donatello, are among the statuary placed in the *loggia*. The building was erected for the use of the Priori, and from it they witnessed all great spectacles that took place in the square. It derives its name from the guard of foreign soldiers that Cosimo I. established in quarters hard by. To the east and running south is the great Ufizzi Palace, which contains some of the finest art treasures that Florence possesses.

Dante's house stands in the Via Dante, to reach which one leaves the piazza at the north-east corner, passing the back of the Badia on the way thither. The Badia was the Church of the Benedictines, and is built in the shape of a Greek cross. It is notable for the grandest coffered wooden roof in Italy. Just above the frieze which runs round the top of the walls, a fine series of well-carved brackets carries the first portion of the roof—a flat space beautifully ornate with good arabesques. Deep-set bosses in recesses circulate round the carving beyond this, until they centre in a recess so deeply set that it almost becomes a miniature dome. Heavy brackets support and carry the outward thrust. The miniature dome takes the form of a Greek cross, and from it the whole design springs in a very symmetrical manner. Such a massive wooden ceiling speaks volumes for the constructive art of the day.

Opposite the Badia stands the Bargello, or Palazzo del Podestà. In its courtyard is the well-known outside staircase that, sketched "to death," is to be seen represented in almost every shop in Florence. The palace is the national museum, and among its grand collections the work of the della Robbia family can best be studied. Florence is such a treasure-house in every way that one might wander on from church to palace, and museum to gallery for a year, and then be barely acquainted with what lies behind its walls.

Florence, too, was the home of the Renaissance, and although Giotto preceded the great master of early Renaissance, Brunelleschi, his famous Campanile is more classic in style than Gothic. The accompanying sketch was made towards twilight when a day's heavy rain had cleared off. The general impression one carries away of the beautiful bell tower is that of a white mass rising majestically above the congested traffic of the noisy street below. The year 1334 saw the commencement of Giotto's design. His death, however, took place when the work had but reached the first storey of the five. Taddeo Gaddi and Francesco Talenti carried it on, and to the latter are due the windows of the upper storeys. Small lozenges in the lowest depict the Development of Civilised Man from the Creation. Above these is a series of sculptures, and in niches yet higher up are the Prophets, Evangelists, Patriarchs and Sibyls. Giotto intended to add a spire to the heavy balcony which projects from the top of the last storey. The whole structure is cased in white, pink and green marble, and thus harmonises with the exterior of the Duomo which it adjoins. Had the spire been added, the *campanile* would not have the rather top-heavy appearance it has when seen from some distance away.

Figure 31: THE CAMPANILE, FLORENCE

THE CAMPANILE, FLORENCE

The cathedral is a building that stands on the site of a very early church dedicated to S. Salvadore. Appropriately named Sta Maria del Fiore, the construction was commenced in 1298 from the designs of Arnolfo di Cambio. Many hands worked for nearly two centuries at Arnolfo's designs, and continually altered them. On the whole, whatever its merits, the building cannot be said to be an architectural success. The façade, completed as recently as 1887 by Emilio di Fabris, is perhaps the most fortunate feature. The Gothic windows on the north side are certainly very beautiful. The mass of the huge dome seen from the corner of the Via del Orviolo piles extremely well above the domes of the apse and south transept. But most of the good points of the exterior are lost in the "noisy" pattern of the different coloured marble panels, which, like those in Giotto's *campanile*, encase the whole building.

The interior is vast and empty, and the dull grey colour that covers the walls is almost worse than whitewash. Four immense bays constitute either side of the nave. The heavy piers that support the arches would be better without the ugly caps above the capitals. There is a gallery above with pointed arches, and four circular windows on each side form the clerestory. The best portions of the interior are the two aisles. The glass in the windows of these, although almost obscured by dust and cobwebs, is very lovely. The interior of the great dome was painted by Vasari and Zuccaro, but reveals no beauties of design. The High Altar is situated beneath this, and the choir stalls which are around are enclosed by a high marble screen. Under the altar, in a fine bronze casket, lie the remains of S. Zenobius, who was bishop of Florence at the end of the fourth century. The apse of the cathedral consists of five chapels; the middle one is dedicated to the saint. Behind the High Altar is a fine, though unfinished *Pietà*, the last work commenced by Michael Angelo. He intended it for his own tomb, but died before it was completed. There are many things of value in both the Sagrestia della Mese, the beautiful bronze doors of which are by Michelozzo, and the Sagrestia Vecchia, over the door of which is one of Lucca della Robbia's very best works. It is true that with oft-repeated visits the vast building grows on one, but, however much its size may impress, it cannot be called a landmark in Italian architecture.

Close by these two structures and due west of the cathedral façade, in the middle of the Piazza del Duomo, stands the Baptistery. Its eight walls were covered with marble by Arnolfo di Cambio some time after the west door had been removed and the rectangular space for the altar constructed inside. The three doors that remain are, with the lintels, superb examples in bronze of the Renaissance period. The twenty panels which depict the life of S. John the Baptist on the south door are the work of Andrea Pisano. At the base of one lintel two nude male figures carry children at a vintage festival; at the base of the other are two female figures, amidst a cluster of corn stalks. Andrea

Pisano has almost excelled himself in the exquisite foliage which grows up both posts. Above the door is a bronze group in which S. John kneels to receive the stroke from the executioner's sword, while an angel holds up a hand shielding the sight from her eyes. The East door by Ghiberti contains prophets and sibyls in niches between the ten panels that illustrate episodes of the Old Testament. The third door is by the same hand. Its twenty panels of Gospel history are surrounded by exquisite foliage, amidst which snails and beetles crawl and bees suck honey, while here and there the fascinating head of an impudent little frog peeps out.

The interior does not compare with Pisa's Baptistery. Granite columns with gilt Corinthian capitals support a triforium gallery composed of round arches with Ionic pillars. The square lights of the clerestory, which alternate with mosaic panels, are behind another gallery that leans inwards. From this springs the mosaic-covered dome. Up to the year 1571 a large font stood in the centre, directly under the opening in the middle of the dome, which until then had no cupola. It was moved in that year by Francesco I. for the baptism of his son! An act of sacrilege which speaks volumes for the absolute power of the autocratic grand dukes of those days.

Figure 32: PONTE VECCHIO, FLORENCE

PONTE VECCHIO, FLORENCE

It is very interesting to examine the almost interminable series of portraits that hang on the walls of the long passage connecting the Ufizzi and Pitti Palaces. This passage crosses the river, and may be seen in the illustration of the Ponte Vecchio, with its square barred windows looking up the river. It is above the jewellers' shops—a favourite haunt of the tourist—that hang so airily like spiders over the water and crowd the old bridge. Amongst this extraordinary collection of portraits of the Medici and their collaterals, may be seen one of our own Charles II., Eleanor of Toledo, wife of Cosimo I., and Catherine de Medici, whose sly eyes, cunning and cruel mouth in no way belie her character. All the reigning grand dukes are here, and not one of them can be said, if these are faithful portraits, to have a really open honest countenance. To judge by their physiognomies, they ruled by brute force and craft. However, there are bronze figures of two of the race who in metal appear more like noblemen than these travesties in paint. Indeed when one sees the gilded figures of Ferdinand I. and Cosimo II. standing over their tombs in the Capella Medicea, we feel they were men of the great race that made Florence famous throughout the civilised world.

The Capella Medicea stands at the back of the fine church of S. Lorenzo. It is a gloomy octagonal building with a dome, and lined throughout in a dull and heavy scheme, with most costly marble. The interior of the dome is painted and gilded. Six members of the great family lie here in their sarcophagi. The remains of two more rest in the Sacristy. But it is not in connection with any reverence for the scions of the Medicean House that our footsteps are drawn hither. No, the little sacristy is crowded all day with those who come to see the work of Michael Angelo. Beneath the statue on the tomb of Giuliano de Medici are the colossal figures of Day and Night. These two wonderful creations are surpassed by Dawn and Twilight on the tomb of Lorenzo, a grandson of Lorenzo the Magnificent, and father of Catherine de Medici. His well-known seated figure is on the tomb. More simple than these is the beautiful, but unfinished, group of the Virgin and Child. The little altar, too, is a masterpiece of simplicity by the same great hand.

To the church of S. Lorenzo is attached the celebrated Laurentian Library, which contains the most valuable collection of MSS. in Italy, the Vatican alone excepted. Among these is the seventh-century MS. of the Vulgate Bible, written by Ceolfrid Abbot of Jarrow. At the corner of the Piazza de S. Lorenzo is a fountain surmounted by a statue of Giovanni delle Bande Nere, leader of the "Black Hand," whose son became the Grand Duke Cosimo I. Opposite this fountain is the magnificent palace of the Medici, the Palazzo Riccardi. From its beautiful *cortile*, with reliefs by Donatello, a fine staircase leads up to the big hall that has a ceiling painted by Luca Giordano. The palace was built by Michelozzo for Cosimo, who lavished his wealth to such an extent that the title he acquired of *Pater Patriæ* was perhaps no misnomer. By the same profuse expenditure his grandson Lorenzo became known as Lorenzo il Magnifico. The family of Medici appears in the chronicles of Florence towards the end of the twelfth century; but the first member to lay claim to any distinction was Salvestro, who took a prominent part in the revolt of the *Ciompi* in 1378. The leader of this insurrection was Michele di Landi, a *ciompo* or wool-carder. Giovanni, the banker, amassed the great wealth which enabled his son Cosimo to carry out his ambitions.

Apart from the Capella Medicea the church of S. Croce may be looked upon as the Westminster Abbey of Florence. In it is the tomb of the great master who created "Dawn and Twilight." The monument to Michael Angelo Buonarotti is the work of Vasari. Alas! one cannot but lament that the irony of Fate has ordained the resting-place of genius should stand against a wall on which are painted red curtains! Not only red curtains, but a hideous red canopy with gold tassels drawn aside by vulgar little abominations in the shape of fat cherubs. For once, one longs for the whitewash brush. The cenotaph of Dante is placed close to the beautiful Renaissance tomb of Leonardo Bruni. The recumbent figure of the diplomatist lies stretched out on a slab borne by eagles, and represents real repose in a marvellous manner. The red brick floor of the church is almost covered with tomb slabs, some still in good relief, others worn flat. Among them is that of John Ketterick, Bishop of Exeter, who died in Florence in 1419 when on an embassy for his sovereign.

The airy interior of S. Croce is very fine. Slender octagonal columns of a russet hue bear pointed arches with Italian-Gothic capitals. The aisles have wooden roofs. The glass in the windows is good; and the chapels at the east end and in the transepts are covered with most interesting frescoes by Giotto, Taddeo and Agnolo Gaddi and others. S. Croce is still served by the Black Conventuals, a sub-order of S. Francis. The cloisters attached to the monastery were designed by Arnolfo di Cambio, and through them one reaches the Capella Pazzi, one of Brunelleschi's best buildings. The fine portico with its colonnade of Ionic columns has a frieze of cherubs attributed to Donatello. The entrance to the cloisters is from the Piazza S. Croce, the buildings on the south side of which are typical of old Florence. The upper storeys of these grey-brown walls overhang and are supported by huge wooden cantilevers. One house, the Palazzo di Niccolo dell' Antela, is covered with allegorical paintings by Giovanni da S. Giovanni, and on it is a white marble disc that marked the goal in the game of *calcio*. The Piazza, which is one of the largest in the city, was in bygone days the public games-ground.

Another fine church of one of the great preaching Orders is S. Maria Novella, which stands in the piazza of the same name, not far from the railway station. The façade is a very clever adaptation by the genius who planned the transformation of "Il Tempio" in Rimini, Leo Battista Alberti. In S. Maria Novella he fitted Renaissance ideas to the earlier Gothic construction of the arcades and lower portions of the buildings. Like all Dominican churches the nave is disproportionately large, built always thus to accommodate the great congregations who flocked to hear the sermon; and so that all could hear, the pulpit was placed nearer the west than the east end. In the sixteenth century Vasari altered the interior and took away the marble screen that divided the conventual from the public part of the church. It stood where a couple of steps run right across the church at the fourth bay of the nave. This is lofty, with a groined vault and pointed arches. The transepts have lateral chapels and the choir is very shallow. One of these chapels is that of the Rucellai family, whose coat of arms with an inflated sail has been used with as good an effect by Alberti in the decoration of the façade as the Malatesta coat at Rimini, where it will be remembered the little elephants play so important a part in his scheme. In this chapel is the famous panel, the so-called Cimabue's "Madonna," which some critics attribute to Duccio da Siena. Speaking personally, however, I failed to discover the greenish undertones that are a feature in Duccio's work. The story tells us that when the picture left Cimabue's studio it was hailed by the people in the streets with great admiration and holy fervour. Attached to the west wall of the church are the cloisters. The Chiostro Verde, so called from the greenish colour of its frescoes, contains the Spanish chapel. One can here spend a very instructive morning examining the fine mural decorations that cover the walls. The Chiostro Grande is now a military gymnasium; but the upper part is devoted to the Institution for Deaf Mutes and the Society for Repressing Beggars. Many useful articles can here be purchased that are made by the very poor. Tourists, make a note!

There is another useful institution, and one perhaps that is much better known. The Spedale degli Innocenti, or Foundling Hospital, which admits infants without any inquiry, and when the children are old enough boards them out in peasant families, where they are trained to earn a livelihood. The hospital is the work of Brunelleschi. In the spandrils of the *loggia* are the medallions of infants in blue and white by Andrea della Robbia, reproductions of which hang on many a wall throughout the civilised world.

Not far off is the monastery of S. Marco, the cloistered courts of which once ran red with the blood of the monks. Fra Angelico's intensely religious frescoes in the monastic cells surely helped to inspire the brethren to defend their home by force of arms against those who were determined to eradicate every vestige of their beloved Savonarola. A few relics of this great democrat are still to be seen in his cell. The writing-desk he used, a book of commentaries in his own minute hand, his crucifix and other personal objects, remain as silent witnesses of the fierce struggles in a mind brought to the lowest depths of despair and well-nigh prostrate when the last act was accomplished in the Piazza della Signoria.

Of the many great Florentine palaces the two that hold the incomparable collections of pictures are the best known. The Uffizi stands on one side of the river, the Pitti on the other. Emulating the lavish expenditure of their rivals, the Medici, the Pitti family employed Brunelleschi and Fancelli to erect a building which should outshine all the Medicean palaces in Florence. So much was spent on it that eventually the family were ruined, and Fate, that so often plays with the over-ambitious, ordained that their rivals should step in and purchase the huge building. The Grand-dukes of the Medici took up their residence in the building, part of which is now the Royal Palace. From the beautiful Boboli Gardens at the back, a very good view is obtained of the cathedral and Giotto's Campanile, with Fiesole and the mountains in the north rising beyond. But if we wish for a comprehensive impression of

Florence as she lies in the valley of the Arno, we must ascend the hill on the top of which the church of S. Miniato al Monte stands. Beneath the cypress trees at our feet the classic stream, crossed by its famous bridges, winds away in the direction of the Monti Pisani. The great dome of the Cathedral seems almost out of proportion with the lesser landmarks around it. More than ever does one wish to see the spire that Giotto designed to finish his grand bell-tower. And as the eye wanders over roofs and embattled walls, the mind goes back to Medicean days, ignoring for once the utilitarian vandalism that has carried the noisy tramcar through the intricacies of the maze below us in desecration of the memorials of a great age.

Figure 33: THE DUOMO, FLORENCE, FROM THE BOBOLI GARDENS

THE DUOMO, FLORENCE, FROM THE BOBOLI GARDENS

PERUGIA

IN the vicinity of Perugia many remains of Etruscan civilisation have come to light, and part of the old Etruscan city walls still stand. On top of the huge blocks of stone of which they are composed one may also see the defensive superstructure added by the Romans, and above this the red brick of a later date. Wandering in the older parts of the city, where the houses are terraced on the steep hill-slopes and the narrow streets, often burrowing under them, wind sinuously in and out, one is carried right back without an effort into mediæval times. Neither does it require any effort to picture the sanguinary faction fights between the great Perugian families, the Oddi and Baglioni. Niccolò Pisano's last work, the figures on the fountain by the steps of the Cathedral, and the unfinished wall of the building itself, are to-day just as they were in the fifteenth century when these same steps ran red with blood in the accomplishment of the diabolical plot which wiped out a whole family, save one. So tired of these conflicts were the more law-abiding Perugians after this deed, or so surfeited with blood, that the might of the Church Militant was called in to put an end to all distracting feuds. The advent of Pope Paul III. was looked upon at the time as a real deliverance; but the crafty Pontiff, knowing the hornet's nest he came into, was sagacious enough to build for himself a fortress-palace in an impregnable position. This, the Rocca Paolina, stood partly on the ground at the end of the Corso Vannucci where a big hotel is now, and on the garden space in front of it. The visitor to Perugia can never forget the incomparable view from the wall of this garden; nor wonder, when he looks over the veritable precipice beneath it, that the Baglioni, whose palace was demolished to make way for Paul's fortress, could hold in terror the rest of Perugia from the security afforded by their own walls. Perugia is like an octopus, with a central hill on which the Cathedral is situated, and from which long feelers stretch out in all directions. A statue in a public garden at the end of one of these feelers, or, more correctly speaking, promontories, commemorates the expulsion of the Swiss Papal Guard by General Fanti in 1860. The city then joined the newly formed kingdom of Italy and made an end of the Church's supremacy by demolishing the Rocca Paolina.

117

Figure 34: THE CATHEDRAL AND OLD TOWN, PERUGIA

THE CATHEDRAL AND OLD TOWN, PERUGIA

It is rather extraordinary that when the strife between the nobles of Perugia was at its height art was in the most flourishing condition. Fashion, or perhaps the hall-mark of the "gentleman" of those days, dictated that he should patronise art. We see this in the records of all the great families of the fourteenth and fifteenth centuries; and however bloodthirsty and revengeful they were amongst themselves, they had this one great merit. And so we find that while the Oddi were slaying the Baglioni, Perugino, Pinturicchio, Raphael, and Signorelli were all at work in Umbria, where one half of the people seem to have given up their lives to bloodshed and the other half to the contemplation of sweet-faced Madonnas and paintings of religious fervour.

In the middle of this ancient city stands its Cathedral, but, alas! with no redeeming architectural feature, either outside or within. The exterior reminds one of the tale of the man who, having made a little money, built a house like a cube with windows, telling his friends that when he could afford it he would have the architecture put on. All that can be said about its outer walls is that if the design of pink marble quatrefoil slabs had been carried out and finished, it would have looked even worse than it does now.

The bronze statue of Pope Julius III. on the south façade was erected by the subscriptions of the people to show their appreciation for the restitution of those privileges of which they had been deprived by the builder of the Rocca Paolina. It is placed on one side of a door, and on the other side the pulpit, put up for the use of S. Bernardino of Siena, who came to Perugia to preach peace and allay the feuds of the nobles, is a sort of pendant.

Ten octagonal columns, painted to represent marble, stand in the nave and support the Gothic groined vaulting which springs from gilded Corinthian capitals. The first bay on the south side is enclosed by a good iron grille. Within is the Capella del S. Anello, containing Perugia's most sacred relic, the wedding-ring of the Blessed Virgin. This was filched one day from Chiusi, the pleasant little town where one so often changes trains on the way from Rome. To prevent a repetition of the theft it has, since its arrival in Perugia, been enclosed in a reliquary that can be opened only by fifteen different keys kept by fifteen different citizens. The Capella de S. Bernardino occupies the opposite bay of the north aisle. The choir is a five-sided apse, round which are the canons' stalls of good *intarsia* work. The central of the three windows is almost filled by the organ loft, and the choir gallery is above the stalls. In the north transept a little door in an almost hidden angle of the wall opens out into the cloisters. Of the two courts the inner, with two galleries, is a very picturesque and quiet spot. Creepers come trailing down the walls, flowers in boxes add a touch of colour, and the cooing of doves gave one the idea that here at any rate, in the precincts of a sanctuary, was a haven of rest from the brawling world outside. The Cathedral library has a great treasure in the possession of the Codex of St. Luke of the sixth century. It is bound in silver and written in letters of gold on purple-coloured vellum—a splendid combination.

Not many of Perugia's churches can rejoice to-day in the preservation of their original state. Those attached to the disendowed monasteries are now mostly barracks, and others have been restored or propped up as a consequence of intermittent earthquakes that developed great cracks in their walls. Coming through the Porta Susanna, the lowest part of which is Etruscan masonry put together without any cement, one leaves the ancient city behind, and, turning to the right, sees across the vacant Piazza de S. Francesco the gem of Perugia's ecclesiastical architecture. The little oratory of S. Bernardino stands adjoining the ruined church of St. Francis. The lovely façade of this tiny building is by Agostino Ducci, who built it in marble and terra-cotta. Its two doors are enclosed by a rounded archway, in the tympanum of which is a figure of our Lord in Glory with two archangels. S. Bernardino is beneath. Around him are many angels who sing to the accompaniment of the musical instruments on which they play. Beyond the angels are two rows of cherubims with heavenly faces. The ground colour of the tympanum on which all these delicately modelled bas-reliefs stand was evidently at one time a gorgeous blue and gold. It has faded to a beautiful "broken" cerulean. The jambs of the portal are green serpentine, and contain three figures of angels on each side. They carry implements of husbandry and agriculture. Six panels on the façade have more angels with musical instruments. Arabesques cover the posts of the portal, and laurel is carved on them as well. Four terra-cotta saints occupy niches; under these are scenes in higher relief illustrating events in the life of S. Bernardino. In one he is depicted saving a boy from a watery grave. The delicate pink and warm opaque yellow of the terra-cotta, the white marble and green serpentine, and the exquisite note of blue, with traces over all of faded and half-obliterated gilding, make this gem one of the best pieces of external colouring to be met with in Italy.

Figure 35: THE PORTA SUSANNA, PERUGIA

THE PORTA SUSANNA, PERUGIA

One finds a church situated at the extremity of each of Perugia's promontories. The Romanesque church just outside the S. Costanza Gate is well worth a visit, if it be only to look at its eastern portal. Slender, twisted pillars of marble support the architrave, on which is a central figure of Christ seated in a circle. On either side are the saint with a dove, and a lion with a gryphon. Elegant pilasters are carried from the steps up above the architrave. They are carved with quaint trees growing out of monsters, and support goats and other animals. Leo XIII., when Bishop of Perugia, restored the façade, but very judiciously left this portal alone. Crosses and other Christian symbols in terra-cotta are the fruit of the restoration. On to all these—in fact, wherever they could find a purchase—the mason-bees have settled and built their nests. The drowsy hum from the busy little colony adds much to the pleasure of a reverie as one sits on the steps of the doorway and looks across the vale to Assisi, baking in the sun, and to the scarred mountains beyond.

The never-completed church of S. Domenico, which Giovanni Pisano designed as a Gothic building, contains a grand Gothic monument by that master. The figure of Pope Benedict XI., who died by eating poisoned figs, lies on his sarcophagus behind curtains which two charming figures draw aside. The fine Gothic canopy of the tomb is supported by twisted columns inlaid with *tesseræ* in the same style as the pillars in the portico of Lucca's cathedral.

The Benedictine church of S. Pietro would have been a very impressive basilica had not every inch of its walls been covered by poor frescoes and huge canvases of mediocre paintings. The nave is simple, with a good coffered roof. In one of the aisle chapels there is a very beautiful altar by that delightful artist, Mino da Fiesole; and the tabernacle over the high altar is a good example of marble work. It is surmounted by bronze figures standing at the angles round the base of its little cupola. The magnificent reading-desk is also worthy of note. It rests on a table with good carved panels illustrating events in S. Peter's life.

Figure 36: THE PIAZZA GARIBALDI, PERUGIA

THE PIAZZA GARIBALDI, PERUGIA

One of the finest Domestic Gothic façades in Italy is that of the Palazzo Pubblico. A grand doorway of clustered and twisted columns ornamented with arabesques gives on to the Corso Vannucci. Above the portal are the city's three protectors, SS. Lorenzo, Ercolano, and Costanza. By their sides and overhanging the pavement, on brackets, are two huge gryphons holding a sheep and a calf. Within the building are the Municipal Offices, and on the third floor the *pinacoteca*, on the walls of which hang some of Perugino's best work. The façade, which faces the Piazza del Duomo, has a fine flight of steps leading to an entrance on the first floor. Above this are two more gryphons in bronze and a lion. Depending from the gryphons is the great chain and bar which were captured from the Sienese. Three fine arches support a *loggia*, outside which is a pulpit, removed hither from the demolished church of S. Salvatore. This side of the Palazzo is the oldest part of the building, preceding in construction that which is in the Corso Vanucci by fifty years. A third part, that was added in 1429 for the Bankers' Guild, is known as the Collegio del Cambio. The great hall inside is decorated with very good examples of Perugino's brush, and has a marvellous ceiling covered with arabesques and medallions by his pupils. Carved stalls and benches of walnut wood with *intarsia* work, and fine doors, complete an *ensemble* which is one of the best examples of an early Renaissance interior.

The old Piazza del Sopra Mura, so called because the buildings on one side were erected on the Etruscan walls, has been renamed the Piazza Garibaldi.

A statue of the hero may be seen in the illustration. On the right of the sketch, built on the walls, is the Palazzo del Capitano del Popolo, at present the Assize Court. Its Gothic façade has a good porch and a *ringheria*, or balcony. The *piazza* is one of the best "bits" in this quaint old city, and when filled with market folk haggling over bargains under their umbrellas is a typical Italian scene in a typical Italian setting.

There are not many places in Italy that boast so fine a view as Perugia can from the garden where once stood the Baglioni's palace. In winding lines directly beneath one a road, buttressed up by great blocks of masonry, now leads downhill to the station. To our left is a mat of grey-brown roofs, out of which rise hundreds of curiously shaped chimneys. Heavy stones keep some of the roof tiles in place. A necessary precaution, for, although these are laid three deep, a storm of extra violence is apt to whisk them away by scores. Glimpses of delicious walled-in gardens and old conventual courtyards nestling behind high walls break the colour of our brown mat with relieving patches of green. Bell towers and a spire or two rear themselves out of the harmoniously coloured network and catch the early sun like beacons. Tortuous alleys appear and disappear amidst this delightful chaos, and little figures like ants may be seen labouring up the steep slopes. A sudden jump in colour from brown to green and the eye has leapt a thousand feet or more to the vast and fertile plain beyond. Shadows thrown by fleecy clouds, with which from our height, we seem to be on a level, chase one another over the emerald carpet. Little hills, covered with trees, appear as flat as the plain below. Dark cypresses and pines cluster round the farms and homesteads that punctuate the landscape with white dots. Long thin ribbons of the same colour tell where the main roads run to Assisi, to Foligno, to Rome or Orvieto. As the eye travels on, the emerald merges imperceptibly into green of a blueish tinge. Hills twenty miles away rise in a purple mass under the shadow of the clouds above. But what a perfect canopy the sky is! The sun pierces the well-ordered battalions that are moving across it from the west, and with long, straight rays strikes the windings of the river that runs on to the Eternal City and flows out to sea. Far away, through the yellow haze that throws the purple hills into such bold relief, are shadowed forms rising tier above tier in the mystery of distant sunlight. The snowy crests of Italy's central chain toss themselves up to heaven, hardly distinguishable from the farthest mass of the marching hosts of the sky. Yes, truly an unforgettable view, and one which the Baglioni of old, from their castle windows, must have drunk in with pride. Well nigh as far as their eye reached the country owed them allegiance.

ASSISI

OF all the wonderful hill towns of Italy, Assisi can claim a kind of pre-eminence in saintship and monasticism. The delicate finger of time has touched lightly and lovingly the little mediæval fortress which gave to the world S. Francis and S. Chiara. One might say that every stone in the place is saturated with the memory of the former and sweetened by the recollection of the saintly woman who outlived him many years. The life of S. Francis of Assisi is one of the most enthralling tales in the history of the saints. He, who was the son of a rich cloth merchant, and up to the age of twenty-four had led a gay and vicious life, has left to humanity one of the greatest examples of charity, humility and chastity that the world has ever seen.

As one approaches the quiet little place, the first thing to attract is the great church of S. Maria degli Angeli, built over the Porziuncula. This, a small chapel, was presented to S. Francis by the Benedictines of Mte Subacio, and is the scene of the closing years of his life and his death. A fine altarpiece by Andrea della Robbia in the north transept shows the saint receiving the *stigmata*, or wounds of our Lord's Passion. Pope Pius V. raised the cupola that is directly over the spot where S. Francis expired. The charming little garden where the saint cultivated his plants and medicinal herbs adjoins the sacristy; and there still flourish in it the thornless roses of the legend. Two years after the death of S. Francis, the immense building that rises on a massive substructure was commenced by Gregory IX. The great convent and two churches, one above the other, that seem from below as solid as the rocks beyond, were erected over the saint's grave. S. Francis, when dying, expressed a wish to be interred outside the city walls; but his disciples, so we are led to believe, carried his body up secretly two years later, and placed it in a sarcophagus, which was found imbedded in the rock in the year 1818. It had lain there inviolate for six hundred years.

The lower church, which one enters by a Gothic porch, is very dark. This is emphasised if the sun happens to be very brilliant. By degrees, however, the wonderful ultramarine used in the decoration of the groined roof asserts itself, and what at first seemed utter blackness unfolds imperceptibly into an extraordinary scheme of colour. The costly blue was presented by Hecuba, Queen of Cyprus, whose tomb is in the church. The great porphyry vase in which it was brought thither is there too. Chapels raised six steps above the floor of the nave take the place of aisles; and their windows, filled with stained glass, do not help to mitigate the darkness. The High Altar stands at the inter-section of the nave and transepts. Immediately beneath is the rock containing the saint's remains. The altar itself is a huge slab of stone brought from Constantinople. It rests on twenty slender columns that form a sort of arcade with trefoils and mosaic spandrils. The tour compartments of the vault above are adorned with some of the finest of Giotto's work. They are known as the Poverty series, and Chastity, Obedience, and S. Francis in Glory.

A fine vestibule at the west end of the nave fronts the Piazza Superiore, and carries the façade of the upper church. This is smaller than the lower church by the width of the side chapels, and consists of a nave, short transepts, and apse. The nave is decorated by a once noble series of frescoes by Giotto of the life of S. Francis. They are much damaged by injudicious restoration, and comparing them with other works by the same master-hand, it is open to question whether much of the colour from his brush is now on the walls. Above them is the almost ruined work of Cimabue. Alas! that such masterpieces should have been so neglected.

On the way to the upper town one passes through the old Roman Forum, now the Piazza Grande. In the square stands the Palazzo del Capitano, to which a fine tower is attached. Further on, as one climbs the ascent, the street opens out into the Piazza Rufino, at the end of which the cathedral is situated. Dedicated to the first bishop of Assisi, who suffered martyrdom in the year 286, the building was commenced in 1140. The fine façade has three portals, elaborately carved in low relief, and three very good round windows. Grotesque figures of birds and beasts are set on brackets near the centre window, and occupy other places on the façade. The interior was restored and altered at the end of the sixteenth century, and is in no way remarkable. It contains, however, the font in which S. Francis was baptized, and two good statues of white marble, one of S. Francis, the other of S. Chiara.

Figure 37: THE CATHEDRAL, ASSISI

THE CATHEDRAL, ASSISI

Assisi is distinctly a sun-baked city; and built of local warm-coloured stone, it looks almost on fire when the rays of the setting sun light up its walls, its roofs, and its towers. Thus does the illustration depict the cathedral's façade and Romanesque *campanile.* In the piazza stands, on a pedestal, the bronze statue of the saint which replaced that which is inside the building. The street under the houses on the left leads to the Roman theatre, and on the right one proceeds to the church of S. Chiara. The mummified body of S. Clare still rests in the crypt; and the Crucifix which spoke to Giovanni Bernardone in the church of S. Damiano is in the north transept. To this crucifix was due the change which transfigured the life of the young man, and gave to the world one of its greatest saints. Giovanni was nicknamed Francesco by his father, who had an extensive trade connection with France, and a name given in jest has become one of the most remarkable in the history of the Church. The country round Assisi is full of beautiful subjects for pen and pencil; and long meditative rambles are within reach of the poorest pedestrian. The spirit of S. Francis dominates all. It is not far to the *carceri*, the little dug-out rock chambers that he at first inhabited with his few followers; and the gorge through which one climbs to reach them is that where he was one night attacked by robbers, who finding their victim clad only in a hair shirt, beat him and left him for dead in a drift of snow. The life of S. Francis has ever been an all absorbing one for the painter's art. One of the favourite subjects connected with it is his marriage with the Lady Poverty. The vows he took of Poverty, Chastity and Obedience were demanded from all his followers. His rule once established, his disciples were known as the Frati Minori. When preaching to the poor he often exposed to view a representation of the birth of Christ which he carried about, and it was over this *presépio*, or manger, that the first Christmas carols were sung.

SIENA

SIENA, the Ghibelline, at one time always at war with Florence the Guelph, no longer disputes with her ancient rival the glory of being the foremost of Tuscan cities. But, though she no longer does this, pride in her Roman origin has never ceased. She still retains the S. P. Q. S. as the head-line of municipal notices; and the she-wolf and twins are to be found sculptured on many a column that adorns some of her little courtyards as well as on odd corners about her walls. Nine gates, one of which boasts a barbican, admit the stranger to her dark up-and-down-hill streets. She possesses many fine palaces. She might have possessed the grandest Gothic cathedral in all Italy had funds permitted its completion. As it is, it is one of the most remarkable and is adjoined by one of the most beautiful *campanile* in the country. If the visitor braves the heat of August, she can show him the very best survival of mediæval times in her celebrated *Palio*, or horse-race, that takes place every year in the great piazza. In her streets you will hear the purest Italian spoken. Her women, as the month of May comes round, don the most becoming of straw hats, and her people are justly famed for their courtesy. Fortunately for some of us, the tourist hurries on to Florence or Rome. But for him who loves the repose and personal charm of an old-world city, Siena will always open her arms and gather him in an embrace that will hold him for ever enchanted by the fascination of a delightful memory.

Almost in the centre of the city and occupying a space on the top of the highest hill, Siena's cathedral is to-day a fragment only of what its builders hoped to erect. The west end of the original nave is away at the end of the piazza to the south of the present south transept. The present nave was built as one of the transepts, and when its size is realised the grand scheme that was never completed can be judged. The building was begun in 1229 and the dome over the crossing finished thirty years later. About sixty years after this the scheme to construct the huge nave was commenced. It was only owing to a terrible plague which carried off, it is said, eighty thousand people, that this was abandoned. The tracery of a very beautiful Gothic window remains at the unfinished west end, to make one marvel at the splendid proportions of the intended fabric.

Figure 38: THE CATHEDRAL, SIENA

THE CATHEDRAL, SIENA

The cathedral, of which a fine view is obtained from the church of S. Domenico on the opposite hill, is approached from the Piazza del Duomo by twelve marble steps. The topmost which forms the platform in front of the façade is inlaid with *graffiti* designs in black and other colours. Three crocketed gables crown Giovanni Pisano's façade. Their surface is covered with modern mosaics. Under the centre gable, surrounded by a square frame of Gothic niches filled with half-length figures of saints, is an immense round window devoid of all tracery, but filled with good glass. A flat black band of marble frames the niches. Elegant turrets with crocketed pinnacles surmounted by saints are on either side of this gable. The two other gables are flanked by towers, each with a solid turret. The purest piece of architecture is the gallery which is between the centre and these two side gables. Below runs a classic frieze separating the upper from the lower part of the façade. The columns and pilasters of the three portals are of white and red marble; they are so heavily laden with elaborate sculpture of beasts, birds, and foliage that they seem to lose their *raison d'être* and no longer support anything. The capitals of all these are formed of elongated acanthus leaves, and might be likened to a field of waving maize. It is very interesting to note, by the classic work which Pisano introduced everywhere on the façade, how difficult it apparently was for him to get away from the tradition of his country's classic architecture when designing a Gothic façade.

The whole front is covered with white marble statues perched on every available place. Gargoyles, like *chevaux de frise*, protrude from every angle and corner. On the brackets over the four main columns of the porches are two horses, a winged lion, and a lion *regardant*. The whole of the front lacks repose, a condition which is intensified by the black and white inlay of the flat surfaces. The centre gable overlaps the portal beneath, and the apexes of the two side gables are beyond the middle of the two side portals. This is a good arrangement, and assists the balance of the composition, which is well restrained by the deep-set gallery and dark shade of the flanking towers.

The pointed windows of the south aisle and transept are canopied. On top of each of the buttresses between them is a white marble figure. The magnificent *campanile* rises above the chapel close to the south door. Like the rest of the cathedral it is banded in black and white marble. The lowest of its seven courses is constructed with a solid exterior, the next is pierced by an arch, the third by two arches, and so on, increasing until at the top stage there are six arches. Four turrets with slender spires finish off the corners at the top, and a good hexagonal spire rises from the centre. The dome is supported by an open gallery. The idea of a central tower never seems to have appealed to the Italian in his Gothic work; even at Milan the spire of the cathedral can hardly be said to rise from a tower.

The interior of the cathedral, by reason of the very decided black and white bands of marble, although mellowed with age, is not restful to the eye. The nave consists of five bays on each side. The aisles have round arches. The transepts are double and of unequal length. All the windows are pointed with the exception of the two round ones at the east and west ends. The clustered columns of the nave are of very good proportion; above them is a heavy frieze. Between the numerous consoles of this is a series of terra cotta busts of all the Popes. Executed at one time, they are, like the medallion portraits of the Pontiffs in S. Paolo fuori at Rome, not authentic likenesses. What gilding there is, is away up in the roof and on the bosses in the soffits of the arches, but it is old and not really obtrusive. The same may be said for the star-spangled blue vault. The illustration shows the cold light from the north transept window striking Niccolò Pisano's beautiful pulpit, in contradistinction to the warm rays that penetrate this noble fabric through the clerestory windows of the nave. Arnolfo di Cambio and Niccolò's son Giovanni had a share in the execution of this splendid work, which may be ranked next to the pulpit in the Baptistery at Pisa. The pavement of the whole cathedral is composed of *graffiti* in coloured marble pictures. To preserve this unique pavement the authorities have wisely covered the nave and aisles with a wooden floor; and except during the month of August and on great festivals, when this covering is taken away, the only portion in the lower part of the church exposed to view is that under the dome. This is railed off.

The six niches at the top of the clustered columns that support the cupola are filled with colossal metal figures. On bronze brackets, fixed to each pier of the choir, are thirteenth-century bronze figures of angels holding lamps. One admires the good taste that has always left these bronzes ungilded. The same praise may be accorded in the case of the grand bronze candlesticks on the high altar, and the magnificent tabernacle by Lorenzo di Pietro which rests on it. The only note which really jars is the crescent of hideous gilded cherubims that partially surround the east window. The choir stalls, which were exchanged for those in the convent of Mont' Oliveto Maggiore, nineteen miles out of Siena, have extremely good *intarsia* work of architectural and "still-life" panels.

Figure 39: INTERIOR OF SIENA CATHEDRAL

INTERIOR OF SIENA CATHEDRAL

In the north aisle is the Piccolomini chapel, with a very fine Renaissance wall of carved arabesques. In niches stand statuettes, in the execution of which Michael Angelo had a hand. The celebrated Libreria Piccolomini adjoins this. Its walls are decorated with the frescoes of the life of Pius II., a scion of this noble House. In the centre of the library stands the beautiful group of the Three Graces, a Græco-Roman work which Raphael drew from and studied.

The baptistery, S. Giovanni Battista, is below the east end of the cathedral on a steep hill-side. Its exceptionally good Gothic front by Giacomo di Mino was never completed, and for this reason, as will be seen in the illustration, the roof of the cathedral has a barn-like termination at this end. The interior is a sort of transverse nave with two piers supporting a groined and vaulted roof. The frescoes of the apse, though much faded, still retain some of the rich colouring with which two Brescian painters decorated them. The font is a very beautiful example of Giacomo della Quercia's work, and is adorned with six bronze gilt panels, one of which is by Donatello. Small figures occupy the corners, and are by the same master-craftsman.

Among the many great names on Siena's roll of fame, the two saints Catherine and Bernardino are perhaps the best known. A little way beyond the margin of the first picture of this chapter, to the left, is the house where the former first saw light. The last of twenty-five children born to Giacomo Beninsca and his wife, her childhood was marked by an extraordinary ascetic devotion overwhelming all other feelings, so that at the age of sixteen she entered the Order of S. Dominic. The series of chapels which the Casa Beninsca is now turned into will be for some, from their sacred associations, the most interesting spots in all the city. The house has a charming *loggia* and *cortile*, but otherwise no architectural features worthy of note. On the hill above, and behind the spot from which the sketch was made, is the church of S. Domenico, in which S. Catherine worshipped; it is a huge building in the style of all Dominican churches, with a great nave, no aisles, a shallow choir and transepts. Her life was one replete with visions. In the chapel at the west end S. Catherine took the veil. Little could she have known at the time, that she was ordained some future day to be the prime factor in recalling Pope Gregory XI. from Avignon to Rome.

S. Bernardino was the son of the Governor of Massa Maritima, a Sienese town not far from the coast opposite the Isle of Elba. He joined the preaching Order of S. Francis at the age of twenty-two, and was one of those who always drew immense crowds to listen to his eloquent words. When in Florence he made a bonfire of evil books and vanities, thus forestalling one of Savonarola's great revolutionary acts. So great was his influence considered to be that, while in Perugia, the great bell was always tolled during his occupation of the pulpit. Care of the poor was one of his chief aims, and he established the "Monte di Pietà," for lending money on small pledges, to save those in want from the heavy hand of the usurer.

Of all the palaces in Siena that which stands on the south side of the

Campo, the Palazzo Pubblico, is the most famous. Nearly every one who reads these lines must be familiar, through photographs or otherwise, with the magnificent *campanile* "del Mangia"—a title that originated with a figure, nicknamed the "Glutton," that at one time struck the hours on its bells. The illustration gives a view of the tower seen through the Arco di S. Guiseppe. It is three hundred and thirty-four feet high, and is built of brick with a machicolated stone cap and bell-turret above. At its base stands the Cappella della Piazza, a very beautiful open *loggia*, built to commemorate the city's deliverance from the great plague that was instrumental in causing the proposed enlargement of the cathedral to be given up. The Palazzo itself consists of a huge central square block with Sienese battlements—square with hatched mouldings. A couple of turrets rise in three storeys above the two side wings of the block. The lowest storey of the building is of stone, the others of that delightful red brick which charms the painter's eye, and is peculiar to Siena. All the windows of the palace are pointed, with a flat containing-member outside the three lights of each. Two good courtyards give entrance by stairways to the upper floors of the building, which is now used for judicial business. Almost opposite, across the Campo, is the Palazzo del Governo, formerly the palace of the great Piccolomini family. It contains the treasures of Siena, the state archives; and in front of it stands the Font Gaia.

In the Via del Capitano, leading into the Piazza del Duomo, is the Palazzo Squarcialupi. This thirteenth-century building was, in the old days, the official residence of the Judges of Appeal and the Captains of War. The Loggia dei Mercanti was built in the fifteenth century for the use of the City Fathers who assembled here in their business capacity of merchants to judge trade disputes. So widespread was the fame of this impartial tribunal that foreigners often brought their differences before it for adjustment. The palace is now known as the Casino dei Nobili. Many fine residences line the tortuous and shady thoroughfares, and others form parts of the different squares. Most of them have iron rings and brackets let into their walls similar to many of the Florentine palaces and those already mentioned in the chapter on Bologna.

Figure 40: THE ARCO DI S. GIUSEPPE, SIENA

THE ARCO DI S. GIUSEPPE, SIENA

It is not, however, so much in the individual buildings that the charm of Siena lies, nor in the long line of painters whose works are on the walls of the Spedale in the Piazza del Duomo, in the Accademia delle Belle Arti, and elsewhere. Rather is it in the personal and intimate note of the beautiful old city taken as a whole. For even the sojourn of a single week will captivate and make one feel as if he belonged to Siena, and Siena to him. It may be that the wheeled traffic, which can follow but two or three distinct lines through her streets, shuts off in silence large areas of the city, and that the visitor is left more to himself and his reveries than is the case in most Italian towns. Whatever it be, it is difficult to define, but the more one knows Siena the more whole-heartedly does one give oneself up to her charm.

Is there anything quite the same, quite so peaceful, and yet so full of history's wars, as the view from the pleasant gardens of La Lizza? Pass on to the walls of the Fortessa at the end of "the Lists," or old tilting-ground, and what a beautiful landscape unfolds itself! Undulating ground, covered with vines and orchards, carries us into a middle distance of cypress and pine-clad hills. These stretch away into an opalescent haze, out of which to the north and east rise the peaks of far-distant mountains. To the west but one great mass soars above the sea of golden mist—Mte. Amiata, always different yet always the same. A solitary mountain, once seen ever remembered; a mountain one can love. What a land of sunshine and pastoral beauty it is! Always at its best in springtime before the summer's sun has laid its grip on the red earth and scorched it sere, and when the showers of April freshen and draw from the warm soil that scent of Mother Earth, which nothing man has ever made can equal and which no money can buy.

Figure 41: UNDER THE WALLS, SIENA

UNDER THE WALLS, SIENA

ORVIETO

ORVIETO, yet another of the wonderful hill towns of Italy, is quite unlike any of those with which this book has hitherto dealt. It has an absolutely insular position, due to its situation on top of an isolated crag of dark volcanic rock which rises out of the wide valley of the river Paglia. The rock, which crowns the steep slopes of a hill, goes upwards a sheer precipice on three sides. On the fourth, the old road circles and winds in and out of olive groves and orchards, until, having climbed the ascent, it finally enters the city in a bold curve close to where the funicular rail from the station terminates. The principal entrance is the Porta Maggiore at the other end of the rock. It is a gateway hewn out of the solid *tufa* and built across a very narrow natural gorge. Two other gates pierce the walls. One, at the east end, is close to the old Fortessa—now converted into a charming garden. Like an old eagle that in his declining years cannot trust his wings for far flight, this grim old city, built of black lava, broods over the sweep of country below. Very few places in the country occupied so impregnable a position.

On the northern slopes of the hill there has been unearthed in a peasant's garden one of the most complete Etruscan *necropoli* in Italy. One tomb is left exactly as it was found, with the contents—vases, jars, utensils of bronze, &c.—in their original position.

Figure 42: LA PORTA MAGGIORE, ORVIETO

LA PORTA MAGGIORE, ORVIETO

In the troublous times that so often overtook Papal Rome no fewer than thirty-two different Pontiffs found refuge in Orvieto from incipient revolutions. The impregnable situation of the city rendered it safe and immune from attack. Pope Clement VII., who fled here after the sack of Rome by the Emperor Charles V., caused the Pozzo di S. Patrizio to be made. This extremely cleverly constructed well is hewn out of the solid rock for a depth of one hundred-and-eighty feet, and has a double spiral staircase outside the water shaft. The Papal Court naturally followed the Pope, and Orvieto in the days which have gone must have worn a more human air than it does now. One can understand that then its dark, solemn streets resounded with a little gaiety, and its palaces had a greater show of life than they have at the present time. True, the owners now spend most of the year in Rome, and reside in their fortress homes for the summer months only. But even their advent does not, to the stranger, bring much more life into this solemn place. No other word describes the palaces of Orvieto better than the above. Nearly every one of these fortress palaces has a tower of defence, the walls of which are from eight to ten feet thick. Many of them are connected with one another by underground passages, and none have any windows at all accessible from the outside. The lower class of inhabitants are quiet and sad-looking. They appear even to this day to live under some heavy mental weight. Maybe generations of suppression and the dominance of an intriguing Court has had an influence that is inbred into the children born now. Then, too, it was so far down hill and up across the opposite slopes to the world beyond! So toilsome a climb to return home! You feel this to-day when you live in Orvieto—feel that this silent city is an island. Can you be surprised, when you think of these adverse influences, that the poorer Orvietans have not quite the gay and friendly air of the peasantry of the plains? But whatever the people may be, they live in a wonderful old city, and they live under the shadow of a grand Gothic cathedral.

Standing in a fine open piazza with the Palazzo del Papa on one side, the Hospital on another, and the Bishop's palace on a third, this fine church occupies the vantage ground of Orvieto. In the Vatican, one of Raphael's well-known frescoes illustrates the miracle of Bolsena. It was to commemorate this that Pope Urban IV. founded the cathedral. The magnificent façade has three porches. The centre one has round arches, and the other two are pointed. Four flat panels are at the bases of the shafts that divide the façade. These shafts end in crocketed pinnacles surrounding the Gothic turrets, which soar upwards beyond the three gables at the top of the façade. The gables themselves rise above the roofs of the nave and aisles. The only fault one can find with this beautiful building, and it is one common to most Italian Gothic churches, is that the façade is "stuck on," and does not really form part of the architectural composition of the building. A glance at the illustration will explain what is meant.

The four panels are justly placed among the masterpieces of Italian sculpture of the thirteenth century. Vasari attributes the designs to Niccolò Pisano. This may be, but it is known that Giovanni Pisano and others were the artists who executed them. The first in order begins at the lowest left-hand corner of the north panel, and records the Creation of the World and all beasts and birds. Then follow the histories of Adam and Eve, Cain and Abel, Jubal—making bells, and Tubal-Cain measuring on a scroll with a compass.

Figure 43: THE FAÇADE OF THE CATHEDRAL, ORVIETO

THE FAÇADE OF THE CATHEDRAL, ORVIETO

This completes the first and best panel of the four. Each incident is enclosed by a very beautifully cut and intricate pattern of the vine. The second panel depicts scenes from the Old Testament; the third, the Tree of Jesse, the Nativity and Life of Christ, with classic foliage intervening. The fourth is very good and represents the Resurrection; here figures of a very Greek type rise from Greek sarcophagi. Saints, Virgins, and the Saviour in Glory surrounded by Apostles also find places on this panel. It finishes in the lowest right-hand corner with a most realistic scene in Hell. Raphael, it is said, came to Orvieto to study these wonderful works.

Immediately above and at the bases of the four shafts are the huge bronze symbols of the four Evangelists. They rest on the *abaci* of the pilasters which form a sort of drip-course right along the façade. Over the centre porch is a bronze tent, the curtains of which Angels draw aside revealing the Virgin and Child seated. The lights, forming the tympanums of the porches, are thin sheets of alabaster. The columns are spiral and twisted, octagonal and quadrangular. Each is set against a different coloured background of black lava, red, white, or grey marble; and each is covered with geometrical mosaic. The wheel window of the façade is beautified with exceptionally good tracing. It is framed by quatrefoils in panels, with the head of a saint in each. On two sides of these, in recessed rectangular niches, are statues of the Twelve Apostles.

At the top of the frame are canopied niches with a row of saints. The whole of this wonderful front is covered by modern mosaics which do not quite fit in with the severe lines of the architecture. Neither does the scheme of colour in which they are executed take its place with the warmth of the marble as well as it might.

The whole of the main building is constructed in bands of black lava and white marble. Semicircular chapels in the aisles break the monotony of the lower portion of the exterior; while the upper is rendered less severe by the pointed clerestory windows, a dripstone and string-course, and a good cornice.

The interior is one of the best in Italy. It was greatly improved when the colossal statues which stood at the bases of the piers were removed, and the side chapels cleared of their altars and rather meretricious adornments. The massive columns of the nave, eight of which are round, four clustered, and two engaged, have capitals that partake of a style far more classic than Gothic. Above the round arches they support runs a triforium gallery. This is open in the nave, and covered at the west end, where it follows the slope upwards of the gables of the aisles. At the east end it is carried over the window, being also covered in here. The windows of the aisles are all filled, or partly filled, with thin slabs of alabaster. The effect of light produced through this thick but comparatively translucent medium is extremely mellow and beautiful.

The short transepts are raised three steps above the nave, and the choir five. A fine red marble balustrade separates the latter from the rest of the church. The open stalls in the choir have some extremely good *intarsia* work. The wooden screen that shuts them off from the nave is a carved mass of most intricate geometrical design. Under the east window is the bishop's throne, backed and surrounded with more good *intarsia*, in which saints and sainted bishops with their symbols most effectively figure. The walls above and around are covered with fourteenth-century frescoes by Pietro di Puccio and Ugolino, both native artists. In their present faded state they harmonise beautifully with their surroundings, to which the colour of the well-worn red marble floor of the cathedral adds a pleasant note.

The work of Luca Signorelli can be better studied in the Cappella della Madonna di S. Brizio than anywhere else in Italy. This chapel practically forms the shallow south transept. In the magnificent frescoes which adorn its walls one can trace the possible influence of this great painter on the works of Michael Angelo. Two panels of the ceiling came from the brush of Fra Angelico. The north transept is almost entirely occupied by the Cappella del S.S. Corporale. The reliquary containing the "Corporal," or linen cloth of the

Miracle of Bolsena, is kept over the altar. This reliquary is a fine piece of silver-gilt work, with two dozen beautiful panels of blue enamel. It was on to this linen cloth that the Blood dropped from the broken Host, and convinced the officiating priest of the Real Presence. Pope Urban IV. had it brought from Bolsena, and commenced to build this magnificent cathedral as a great shrine in which the sacred relic should rest for ever.

Behind the cathedral, that is to the east, Orvieto, not many years ago, was a ruined, broken-down mass of insanitary buildings. Gardens now take the place of what was a plague-spot, and the houses of the city as we find it now occupy barely one-half of the area contained within the walls. In this respect modern ideas have decidedly improved Orvieto. What is left of the old streets is well looked after from the sanitary point of view; and from the artistic, there are not many places in Italy where subjects are to be found in such plenty. The massive Torre del Moro is close to the Piazza del Popolo, where stands the ruined church of S. Domenico. This fine Romanesque structure is entered by a flight of steps at the west end; it is built over a massively constructed crypt, now used as a granary. The mighty arches of this crypt sustain part of the church, but it does not extend beneath the whole of the fabric. One of the numerous arched gateways which are to be found throughout the city intervenes between it and the little buttressed dwelling underneath the east end. From this rises the solid *campanile*. An arcade runs round the whole church. This good feature is composed of round arches, containing small round-headed lights. The outer member of each arch is finished by a broad, flat, square billet, the inner has a cable pattern. Above is a dripstone and string-course.

Saturday sees the piazza crowded with country folk, and it then presents a busy scene. All the rest of the week it is silent and deserted. I was there with my sketch-book one afternoon. A thunderstorm was rolling about in the hills. The air was charged with disturbing electricity. Swifts flew screaming round the ruined church. A kestrel up in the battered old tower cried to her young. The storm crept nearer. Grand cumuli clouds piled themselves higher and higher above the lightning-riven mass of rain-sodden blackness below. A beautiful swallow-tail butterfly, brilliant against the deep purple background, came gracefully sailing across the square into the sunshine. It hovered, now here, now there, like a spirit from another world seeking rest but finding none. Little puffs of wind stirred odd bits of straw and paper about the piazza. Dust began to eddy round and round. A drop of rain fell on to the open leaves of my sketch-book. It was the writing on the wall; so I closed the book and hurried home. For half an hour the heavens emptied themselves on Orvieto. To me a stage-play of some scene in her past was re-enacted in the sky; the passing storm seemed so appropriate to the rugged old city.

ROME

WITH pen in hand one approaches the subject of the Eternal City with great diffidence. The more one's acquaintance with her has ripened, the more does the attempt to write a chapter seem a hopeless task. There are so many Romes—Republican Rome, Imperial Rome, Rome of the Papal supremacy, Christian Rome, Pagan Rome; and then Modern Rome, with a municipality that is fast changing the face of everything. Catering for the tourist in these days of cheap transit does much to alter things. In the end it will defeat its own object, and history will be contained in libraries and museums only. Rome, like London, is fast becoming cosmopolitan. The *perícolo giallo*, or "yellow peril," as the motor post 'bus is facetiously called, rushes through streets where not so long ago solemn processions of the Mother Church wended their way. Building is going on at present with feverish haste. The "boom" of 1880, which ruined many of the wealthy families who speculated in it, does not seem to have acted as a deterrent to others. The great boulevard projected by the powers that be, slowly grows in length. Despite the outcry against such vandalism, an area that might disclose and yield up unknown archæological treasures if properly excavated is being levelled in the sacred names of sanitation and opportunism! The picturesque dwellings that lined the banks of Rome's famous river have disappeared, and the yellow waters of the historic Tiber rush along between massive walls of stone.

Is it possible amid all these rapid changes to realise what Rome has been and is still? No, not on any of her seven hills, not in her streets, nor on her river embankments, not even in her churches, can this now be done. No: to realise the power and majesty of Ancient Rome one must go out into the Campagna, that desolate plain in which she lies. There, where the stupendous ruins of her great aqueducts stretch away in utter loneliness to the distant hills; there, where once a prosperous people dwelt in plenty, and where the only living things likely to be seen now are a statuesque goatherd and his nibbling flock—there, one may gather an idea of the might of ancient Rome. By Hadrian's Wall, which cuts the Borderland of England, one may do the same; and there are none of her ruined outposts, east or west, where her majesty is not more apparent than in the Eternal City herself.

Figure 44: ON THE PALATINE, ROME

ON THE PALATINE, ROME

Up on the Palatine, close to the trees that are seen in the sketch of the Clovis Victoriæ, the Etruscan wall of the first Rome is now in course of excavation. Up there, too, are the remains of the first wall of the Roman city built by Servius Tullius. In the Via Merulana part of a great earthwork with a moat outside can still be seen. Long after Carthage had been practically obliterated by her rival, Rome had extended so far, and attacks from outside became of so great a danger to the inhabitants, that Aurelian found it necessary to build a line of defence which the present walls might be said to occupy. From that time onwards the city grew steadily to a magnificence and power which has never been equalled. She ruled the known world. But it was not until Constantine the Great transferred himself and the seat of empire to Byzantium that the turning-point in her fortunes was reached. Well has the great emperor earned that proud title! From Milan he issued the decree which gave to the much persecuted Christians equal rights with other religions; and even went further, embracing the faith he had befriended.

Many churches lay claim to be the oldest foundation in Rome. S. Pudenziana is said to be the church S. Paul founded in the house of his Senator friend Pudens. Recent excavations under S. Clemente have brought to light early-Christian masonry beneath the Republican and Imperial remains, over which the present edifice stands. S. Prisca is another ancient church; and tradition attributes S. Giovanni in Laterano, S. Pietro, S. Paolo, S. Lorenzo, S. Croce in Gerusalemene, S. Agnese, and SS. Pietro e Marcellino to Constantine's era. The first four of these, with S. Maria Maggiore, were afterwards known as the Patriarchal Churches over which the Pope presided. With S. Croce and S. Sebastiano, they became the seven churches of Rome. In them the Pontiff celebrated High Mass; and they were the principal churches which drew pilgrims from throughout Christendom. In these seven the high altar presents its back to the congregation, for His Holiness celebrates Mass with his face to the worshippers. The Papal supremacy really owed its foundation to Gregory the Great. But it was not until two hundred years after his decease, when on Christmas Day of the year 800, Charlemagne was crowned by Leo III., that the "Holy Roman Empire" became an accomplished fact. Unfortunately for Ancient Rome the Carlovingian period was one of demolition and plunder. Christian zeal cared nought for the beauty of pagan buildings, and many an one was pulled down and a church erected with the material. It was later on however, in the time of the Renaissance, that columns and marble of every sort were used for the adornment of the numerous sacred edifices which sprang up. What was not wanted in construction was ground down to make lime. Banding iron, clamps, bronzes, and every description of metal that was found were thrown into furnaces and melted down. Nothing that could be made use of for building material was spared. The Church could never forget the persecution she had undergone, nor the thousands of martyrs who had died for the Faith. Is it a matter for surprise then—a surprise one must add mingled with great regret—that the glorious buildings of ancient Rome have almost disappeared?

Whichever of all Rome's churches was founded first, there is no disputing the fact that the huge fabric which occupies one side of the Piazza di S. Pietro is the most famous Christian edifice in the world. Bernini's best work, the grand colonnades on two sides of the square lead up in splendid curves to the great façade of S. Peter's. But, so great is the size of the building, so far set back the dome, that it is impossible to realise the immensity of either from any point of view in the piazza. The first church was founded in the year 90 at the place where so many martyrs had suffered death during the time of the tyrant Nero. The Emperor Constantine commenced afterwards the erection of a basilica on this spot, the façade of which Raphael has handed down in his fresco of the Incendio del Borgo. When Julian della Rovere became Pope Julius II., he wantonly ordered the destruction of the church as it then stood. This was done to make way for a greater with which his own name would be for ever connected; and he employed Bramante to design the new cathedral. Hands once more were laid on the buildings of ancient Rome and the construction was begun from its ruins. Except for some of the columns, the whole of the marble work of S. Peter's was, up to the commencement of last century, abstracted from the same source. Bramante's designs were never carried out. The many alterations to which they were subjected after his death led to great dissatisfaction, and in the end Michael Angelo was consulted. All he could do was to reserve as much as possible of the great architect's ground plan, and this is, except for the lengthening of the nave and the addition of the façade, as the great cathedral stands to-day.

The immense *travertine* columns of the façade form part of a portico which is over two hundred feet in length. Above the columns runs an inscription recording that it was put up by the Borghese Pontiff, Paul V. A balustrade, broken by pedestals, surmounts the *cymatium*; on the pedestals are extra-colossal figures of the Saviour (in the centre) and the Twelve Apostles. At either end are groups of *barroque* angels surrounding a circle over which is the Papal Mitre. In one of these circles there is a timepiece. The ceiling of the portico is a fine example of stucco work.

There are five doors which open into the building. The central is of bronze and one of the few things spared by the destroyer Julius when he demolished the old basilica. The doors next to this are those by which one enters the church. In March 1910 the old and very unhygienic leather flaps were removed, and glazed swing-doors have taken their place. The Porta Santa, or door at the north end of the portico, is walled up. It was only opened for the purpose of celebrating a Jubilee, and has been closed since 1825.

Many and repeated visits are necessary to S. Peter's before the size of the vast interior can be in any way grasped. It is only when one is accustomed to the scale of the little human figures walking about and their insignificance in proportion to the whole, that the immense height of even the Corinthian pilasters of the piers becomes apparent. The roof is vaulted, coffered and gilded. It is supported by four piers on each side of the nave. The floor is of coloured marble, and has the measurements of the great churches of Christendom let in with brass at the spot where each would end if measured from the east. Just inside the central bronze door is a slab of porphyry upon which the emperors were crowned. At the base of each pier, as well as in other parts of the church, the colossal statues of the founders of different religious Orders find a place. The last pier on the right has a bronze figure of S. Peter seated, one foot of which is partially worn away by the lips of devotees.

The dome grows upwards from four massive buttresses. Niches above their bases contain figures of SS. Longinus, Andrew, Helena, and Veronica, who holds the napkin with the impress of the Saviour's Face. Under the dome is the *Confessio* of S. Peter, to reach which a double flight of steps leads down. Eighty-nine lamps for ever burn on the balustrade which encloses the well of the entrance; and doors of gilded bronze shut off the niche in which the sarcophagus of the Apostle rests. Soaring high up on four bronze columns ninety-four feet from the floor, the great *baldacchino* rises above all. But so immense is the space under the dome that one has no idea of the height it attains. It was designed by Bernini, and is made partly of the bronze which covered the roof of the Pantheon.

Nothing at all can be said in praise of Bernini's design. The high altar, at which only the Pope celebrates mass, is above the *Confessio* and directly under the cross which forms the apex of this somewhat unsightly mass of metal. The interior decoration of the dome is not in any way striking. Above the four statues of the already enumerated saints are the *loggie*, containing the sacred relics of the lance which pierced the crucified Saviour's side, the head of S. Andrew, a portion of the Cross, and the "Volto-Santo"—the napkin or handkerchief of S. Veronica, which wiped the Lord's brow on the way to Calvary. Four mosaics of the Evangelists are beneath the frieze which carries the drum of the dome; and a series of four each are between the sixteen gilded ribs of the vaulting. In the tribune at the east end of the cathedral is the ancient wooden episcopal chair of S. Peter.

Amongst other celebrated things which S. Peter's contains is the Pietà of Michael Angelo in the Capella della Pietà. The great sculptor has inscribed his name on the girdle of the Virgin—the only occasion on which he has done so. Opening out from this chapel is another, in which is a column, said to be that against which Christ leaned when preaching in the Temple at Jerusalem. Adjacent to this is the tomb of the great Countess Matilda by Bernini. The tombs and monuments of many Popes are to be found in other chapels, but none of them possess any real artistic merit. The best is that of Alessandro Farnese, Pope Paul III. It is by Guglielmo della Porta, and was one of the most expensive to erect. In the crypt, which is divided into two parts, the Grotte Vecchie, and the Grotto Nuovo, are the sarcophagi and fragments of sarcophagi of many other Popes, among them being that of Nicholas Breakspeare, the only Englishman who ever attained the dignity. The sarcophagus of S. Peter, already mentioned, is in the *Confessio*, or shrine of SS. Peter and Paul, which is richly ornamented with gold and studded with jewels.

In the Stanza Capitolare, which is part of the sacristy, are some remnants from the brush of Giotto that at one time adorned the walls of the old *Confessio*. The treasury contains a wonderful collection of jewelled crucifixes and candelabra. Among the latter is to be found the work of Cellini and Michael Angelo. The famous sacerdotal robe known as the Dalmatica di Papa San Leone, and said to be that used at the coronation of Charlemagne, is also kept here. Apart from its sacred interest, the great cathedral of S. Peter's cannot be said to raise any feelings other than wonderment at its size and admiration for its grand proportions. The exterior is disappointing, and many and many a visit must be paid to the interior before wonderment reaches admiration. Just as it is possible to gain the best impression of the power of ancient Rome outside Rome itself, so does one grasp the size of the mighty fabric only when some miles away in the country beyond the walls. Climb the lower slopes of the hills near Tivoli or Frascati, and what does one see? Apparently a level plain, out of which rises far away a marvellous dome. From Tivoli, especially, one sees nothing of the city on the Seven Hills. The line of fir-trees beyond Monte Mario is visible, and maybe, the afternoon sun shining on the distant Mediterranean. But save for the great dome there is nothing to indicate to the eye that the Eternal City lies well within the range of vision. Yet in Rome itself, though it is paradoxical to say so, the dome of S. Peter's in no way dominates anything, albeit that it rises above everything else. The enormous monument in course of erection on the Capitoline appears bigger. Each of the seven hills seems to be of greater altitude. But the former is not so large, and the latter do not reach the same height. Thus, the great church holds her own—but, physically as well as spiritually, one must go outside Rome to realise this.

To return to ancient times, we find an absorbingly interesting link with pre-Christian days sculptured on one of the panels which decorate the interior of the Arch of Titus. The Via Sacra passed under this arch, which was erected to commemorate the taking of Jerusalem. The panel in question has figured on it in bas-relief a procession bearing the seven-branched candlestick and tabernacle which were spoils from the Jewish Temple. This is the only known material proof existing of the former object, and may therefore be justly said to be of surpassing ecclesiastical interest. Through the archway one sees the half-ruined walls of the Colosseum, the greatest amphitheatre in the world. This, too, is of intense religious interest. In the arena hundreds of Christian martyrs were torn to pieces by wild beasts, or butchered to fill the passing hours with amusement for the Roman populace. Pope Benedict XIV. consecrated the interior after erecting gates outside to preserve it from the demolition which up to his day had been going on for centuries. Small chapels were also formed amongst the lower structural arches, and services held where once the walls resounded to the shouts of bloodthirsty spectators. Close by the Colosseum is another fine archway, the Arch of Constantine. This likewise, has an interest apart from its design. It was put up when the great emperor declared himself in favour of the Christian faith. The devout may ponder over the fact that these two arches, so closely connected with Christianity, are still standing, while nearly every other has long since been razed to the ground.

Figure 45: THE ARCH OF TITUS, ROME

THE ARCH OF TITUS, ROME

Away to the south-east of these three buildings the Mother Church of Rome is situated close to the city walls. Here, on rising ground, overlooking the vast Campagna, stands S. Giovanni in Laterano, "omnium urbis et orbis ecclesiarum mater et caput." Dedicated originally to Christ the Saviour, and afterwards in the sixth century to S. John, this fine basilica is of much greater, archæological interest than S. Peter's. The present building dates from the seventeenth century. All that remains of the once attached Benedictine monastery is to be found in the very beautiful cloisters, which are a transition between Romanesque and Gothic. The church itself has a fine eastern façade—it orientates to the west—of five arches with an intervening gallery. In the *atrium* is a statue of Constantine found in his *Thermæ*. The interior of the basilica is simple, with a very good *opus Alexandrinum* floor. The aisles are double, and are separated from the nave by eleven bays on each side. Colossal statues of Apostles and Prophets find places at the bases of the pillars. The transepts and tribune are raised above the body of the church.

In the centre, the high altar is situated under an ornate Gothic canopy. This contains a tabernacle, erected partly at the expense of Charles V. of France, to receive the busts of SS. Peter and Paul which were found amidst the ruins of the older church. A few years ago the tribune was extended and beautifully inlaid with mosaic carrying out a design of the thirteenth century. Michael Angelo is said to have designed the flat ceiling of the nave, and there is a wooden figure of S. John by Donatello in the sacristy.

In the Piazza di S. Giovanni in Laterano stands a building that contains the Scala Santa, a flight of steps from Pilate's palace in Jerusalem, which Christ is said to have ascended. They are covered with wood, and may only be ascended on the knees. Light enters through barred windows, and partly illumines the solemn gloom of this deeply interesting place. At the top of the stairs is the Sancta Sanctorum, on the architrave above which is engraved in Latin: "There is not a place in the whole world more holy." This was the old chapel of the Popes and the only part of the Pontifical palace that the fire of 1308 did not consume. The present Palazzo del Laterano was built on part of the site of that which this fire destroyed. The old palace was the residence of the Popes from the time of Constantine until their migration to Avignon. The building that now enjoys the above title is a museum, wherein are many fine pieces of pagan sculpture as well as other interesting antiquities. The baptistery of the Lateran stands to the west of the basilica. The interior of this octagonal building is simple but not well lighted. Eight porphyry columns support an antique architrave; and eight smaller columns of marble rise from this and support the dome. The font is in the centre of the floor, which is lower than the pavement near the walls. It is of green basalt, and is supposed to be that in which the Anglo-Saxon king Caedwalla was baptised in the year 689. Rienzi bathed in it the night before he summoned the Pope and the Electors of Germany to appear before him for judgment.

Another and more magnificent basilica is that of S. Paolo fuori, which is situated two miles out of Rome on the Via Ostia. It is the grandest of the many basilicas Rome possesses. Constantine erected a *tropæum*, or sepulchral monument over the spot where Lucina buried the apostle's body; and in 386 the Consul Sallustrius by the Emperor's order began to build the church, which was known as the Basilica Ostiensis. The little town that arose around this sacred spot was on the banks of the Tiber, and from its position was subject to raids from the Saracens and other marauders who sailed up the stream. John VIII. in the ninth century enclosed the basilica and most of the surrounding buildings within a fortified wall. For fifteen hundred years this grand church has had as venerated a shrine as S. Peter's. The kings of England were its protectors until the Reformation severed their connection with the Roman creed; and sovereigns from all parts of Christendom came here to worship. On July 17, 1823, the pine roof caught fire and fell into the nave. The heat from the smouldering mass was so great that some of the columns split and the whole fabric was almost entirely destroyed. Pius IX.

presided at a great function in 1854, when prelates from all over the world assisted at the consecration of the restored building. Eighty monoliths of Simplon granite, brought down Lake Maggiore to the river Po and then by sea up the Tiber, sustain the roof of the nave and aisles. A series of Papal portraits form a frieze above them. Magnificent columns of Egyptian alabaster presented by Mehemet Ali, Viceroy of Egypt, support the *baldacchino* over the high altar. The bases of these columns are malachite, and were given by the Czar Nicholas of Russia. Many other portions of this noble church were given by other princes. The dismay and regret at its destruction were universal. The body of S. Paul rests in the *Confessio* beneath the altar. The very beautiful cloisters of the old Benedictine monastery, now a barrack, vie with those at Monreale in Sicily, which are illustrated in another chapter. The noble *atrium* at the west end of the basilica is almost complete, and when it is finished and opened out to the river, S. Paolo fuori will once more take rank as one of the grandest ecclesiastical edifices in Italy. Among the other basilicas of Rome, S. Maria Maggiore, or the Basilica Liberiana, is the largest, and commands a fine position on the Esquiline. S. Sabina on the Aventine, that hill which is still almost entirely covered by gardens, is connected with the Dominican monastery that adjoins it. The church possesses a wonderfully carved wooden door and an orange tree in its court which grew from an orange pip that S. Dominic planted. S. Agnese fuori is close to one of the entrances to the numerous catacombs. Into this church every twenty-first day of January two lambs are brought to be blessed. After the ceremony is over they are presented to his holiness at the Vatican, and then sent to the convent of S. Cecilia-Trastevere. Here the good nuns weave their wool into *palliums*, which are subsequently worn by different metropolitans of the church.

The only Gothic church in Rome is that of S. Maria sopra Minerva. It contains the tomb-slab of Fra Angelico, whose face, rendered in marble, has a very sad and rather austere look. The interior of the church is marble, and it cannot be said that this polished shining surface is desirable for the lines of a Gothic building. Not far from S. Maria is the most perfect pagan edifice in all Rome—the Pantheon. Here again we have a heathen fabric that afterwards became a Christian church. Boniface IV. consecrated the temple, that Marcus Agrippa had built more than six hundred years previously, to S. Maria ad Martyres. Sixteen huge columns of oriental granite form the portico, and the ancient bronze doors still remain. The interior is a magnificent rotunda lighted by a circular aperture in the centre of the coffered dome. Against the walls, in recesses, rest the sarcophagi of Raphael and other painters. Here too, sleeping his last long sleep, lies King Victor Emmanuel II., to whom all Italians owe so much.

Figure 46: S.S. TRINITÀ DE' MONTI, ROME

S.S. TRINITÀ DE' MONTI, ROME

The church best known to foreigners is undoubtedly that which figures in
the illustration, S. Trinità de' Monti. There is nothing about the church itself
to call for comment; but its fine position, above the beautifully arranged steps,
in the middle of what may be called the "foreign quarter," makes it worthy
of note. Close by is the Villa Medici, the French Academy of Rome. At the
base of the steps is the flower market. Until recently Italians had a great
objection to cut flowers in their rooms—they were supposed to be unhealthy.
Through foreign influence this is slowly giving way, and the market is as much
patronised by the Romans as by the residents of other nationalities. Not
many years ago the foot of these steps used to be thronged every morning
by artists' models, who, in the picturesque garb of their native districts, sat
here waiting for a day's hire. The few who still do this have moved off to
the steps of the Greek church in the Via del Babuino, and the flavour of the
Campagna and the mountains they gave to the Piazza di Spagna is now a
thing of the past. Everything changes, everything passes away. The gaily

coloured costumes of the *ciociare*, the peasants from the districts between Rome and Naples—so-called from the *cioce* or sandal they wear—is now never seen. The exaggerated dress of the flower sellers, who pester the foreigner to buy little faded nosegays, is simply worn for the purpose of extracting *soldi* and as a subterfuge for begging. Away up in the mountains beyond Tivoli are two villages, Saracenesco and Articoli. Though they are adjacent the dialect of the inhabitants is different. There is a deadly feud between them. They both provide the artist in Rome with models. Those who come from the last named pose for the figure, but those from Sarecenesco will only sit draped. They still provide the wet-nurses for Roman babies; for the physique of these Sabine villagers is very fine, as fine perhaps as in the days when the Sabine women were carried off by Roman youths.

Beyond the Villa Medici lie the beautiful gardens of the Pincio. From the terrace at the end, on the brow of the hill, one gets the famous view of Rome. The shady walks and well-kept drives of these noted gardens, and those of the adjoining Villa Borghese, are the favourite rendezvous in the evening for Roman society. We must leave this beautiful *pleasaunce* and dive down into the labyrinth of streets below. Nothing probably strikes one so much on a first visit to the Eternal City as the number of fountains and obelisks that are to be found in whichever direction a morning's walk takes one. Rome is the best supplied of any capital in the world with water, and though she has not the thirteen thousand odd fountains recorded by Cardinal Mai in the year 1540, those that remain still flow unceasingly. The Aqua Virgo brought into Rome by Agrippa to supply his *thermæ* at the back of the Pantheon rushes a never-failing supply into the huge Fontana di Trevi. One may sometimes see a Roman of the poorer class drinking furtively from the basin into which the water runs, drinking because he is leaving his native city and wishes to assure a safe return. The Fontana del Tritone is formed by dolphins, whose tails meet to support the coat-of-arms of the Barberini—the fine Palazzo Barberini is close by—and is surmounted by a Triton holding a conch shell to his mouth. In quite another district, down by the river hidden away amidst the narrow streets of the Ghetto, is the little Piazza Tartaruga. In the middle of this charming little square stands the Fontana delle Tartaruga. The design of this beautiful "Fountain of the Tortoises" has been attributed to Raphael. It is certainly worthy of his great name. The bronze figures of the four youths supporting the basin of the fountain are exceptionally good. With one hand each grasps the tail of a dolphin, the other is raised above their heads to assist the struggles of the little bronze tortoises that are endeavouring to crawl over the slippery wet lip of the bowl. The Fontana La Barcassia, in the Piazza di Spagna, a corner of which is seen in the sketch of S. Trinità de' Monti, is no doubt better known than the last named, but there is no public fountain in Rome that approaches in any way the artistic merit of "The Tortoises."

It is but a step from this to the gloomy looking Palazzo Cenci, which recalls the tragedy of Beatrice of that name. Another pace further on and we find ourselves in a recently cleared space with the new Jewish Synagogue standing close to the river Embankment. Here was situated the old Ghetto of Rome, a quarter which is being fast demolished. One certainly cannot regret the disappearance of some of the abominable slums that not so long ago stood where the housebreaker's pick and shovel have been at work. It was but a few yards from the synagogue that the sketch of the Isle of S. Bartholomew and the old Roman Pons Fabricius was made. S. Bartolommeo is the only island on the Tiber in its course through Rome; and the picturesque buildings of the old monastery are the only buildings left, which the yellow river washes, of all those that less than thirty years ago lined its banks. There is a different air about the Trastevere district across the water. It is another city altogether than the one left behind on the other bank. The foreigner is not so much in evidence, we are once again in Italy. Mount the steep ascent of the Janiculum, and from the wide space in front of the colossal equestrian statue of Garibaldi you will get a grand view of Rome, with the Campagna and Alban mountains beyond. From the top of the hill, as one turns northwards, we seem on a level with S. Peter's great dome. One is puzzled once again, when remembering how it really towers above all, to find that it is not of much significance in the view. Nothing of course is seen of the Vatican, which is situated on the other side of S. Peter's. In the illustration of the Cathedral, however, there is just visible the corner which adjoins it.

Figure 47: THE ISLE OF S. BARTOLOMEO, ROME

THE ISLE OF S. BARTOLOMEO, ROME

The Vatican is the largest Palace in the world and contains the vastest and most heterogeneous collection of all. It is quite impossible to enumerate a tenth of the treasures hidden behind its ochre-coloured walls. Neither can one enter here into any description of the Sistine chapel with Michael Angelo's masterpiece, or Raphael's magnificent frescoes in the Stanze and Loggie. We must pass over the famous picture gallery and the antiquities in the Museo Pio-Clementino and the Museo Chiaramonti, simply remarking that the Vatican Museums hold the finest collections in the world. There is one antique in the square outside which deserves a passing notice, and that is the great monolith of granite standing in the centre of the Piazza di S. Pietro. If Rome is a city of fountains, it is also a city of obelisks. This enormous block of stone was brought by Caligula from Heliopolis and placed in the circus of Nero, which occupied so much of the ground on which the great basilica was afterwards erected. Eight hundred men, besides many horses and over forty cranes, were requisitioned to elevate it in its present position. Turning away from the Vatican and diving into the squalid quarters of the Borgo, one comes on to the covered passage which John XXIII. commenced to build in order to afford a safe mode of retreat from the palace to the Castle of S. Angelo. The fortress of S. Angelo was erected by the Emperor Hadrian as his family tomb; and, as such, its exterior was perhaps decorated with statues. The Emperor died in his villa at Baiæ on the Bay of Naples, but his body was brought here, to be joined, as time went on, by the mortal remains of Marcus Aurelius, Caracalla, and others.

The history of the castle is the history of Rome in the Middle Ages. It has many times withstood a siege, and among other vicissitudes fell before the prowess of Totila and his Goths. The sarcophagus of its founder was used as the tomb for Innocent II., and its inverted lid now forms the font in the baptistery of S. Peter's. The streets in the neighbourhood of the castle have undergone an absolute change. Wide thoroughfares and huge blocks of flats cover the ground that a few years ago was a huge slum. The new Courts of Justice face the river, and the embankment in front is now a fine boulevard. We cross the water once more, by the Ponte Margherita, the bridge which is highest up the Tiber, and find ourselves in that fine square the Piazza del Popolo. Above the beautiful terraces that form the precipitous slope of the Pincio, the trees that adorn the gardens stand out against the blue of the sky. At the foot of the terraces is the church of S. Maria del Popolo, erected on the site of the Domitii tombs, the ghost-haunted burial place of the cruel Nero. Adjoining the church is a grand gateway, the Porta del Popolo. Under its arches on the straight road that runs north, the Via Flaminia, marched out of Rome all those legions that went forth to conquer and to extend the bounds of an Empire that has seen no rival.

NAPLES

THE old Greek colony of Parthenope was founded by settlers from Cumæ, and when the islanders of Pithecusæ (Ischia) built their adjoining town of Neapolis, it became known as Palæopolis. Its port was where the harbour of S. Lucia existed up to twenty years ago. Neapolis occupied that part of the present Naples which lies to the east of this. About 400 B.C. the Republic, formed by these two then united towns, allied itself with Rome; and during the height of the Empire's power, her rulers, statesmen, and poets built themselves residences on the shores of the beautiful bay. Augustus did much for Neapolis, and Tiberius sought refuge in that entrancing island, Capri, where to this day his infamies are a byword. Claudius, Nero, Titus, and Hadrian, whose palace can be seen under the waters of the blue Mediterranean near Pozzuoli, have all left traces of some sort or other in and about Naples. Lombards and Normans, Swabians and Spaniards were each in turn drawn hither, allured by the beauty of the situation. Colossal figures in marble of the most famous rulers of Naples occupy niches on the façade of the Royal Palace, and here Roger the Norman, Frederick II., the Swabian, who founded the university, Charles of Anjou, Alfonso of Arragon, Charles III., Joachim Murat, and Victor Emmanuel II. gaze stonily from their retreats at the noisy tram and rushing motor-car.

The Spanish Bourbons were the last to rule in Naples before Italy was united towards the close of the last century. They did much to improve the city but nothing to help its people. Twenty years ago there were still left members of the aristocracy who every year journeyed to Paris to pay their court to Francis II., the last of that race of kings whose reign had ended at the disastrous battle of Gaeta.

Naples, like Rome, changes every year. Modern improvements bring sanitation, but do away with all that is picturesque. All over the world hotels are becoming a great factor in the life of the folk who have spare cash, and Naples, with her splendid water supply and unrivalled position, is not behind in her eagerness to catch the foreigner's gold. Tourists by the thousand reach her by sea, and the enterprising agents who arrange the itinerary pop them into cabs, drive them through the streets, and deposit them at the far-famed Museum, where they are hustled from one gallery to another by the anything but intelligent guide. However, the Museum alone is worth a visit to Naples. The ashes from Mte Somma which smothered Pompeii, preserved for subsequent ages objects in bronze, in earthenware, and in glass, which lie in their cases—an open book of the domestic life of the Roman for every one to read. The great Farnese Hercules, brought by Caracalla from Athens to adorn his baths in Rome, is in one of the lower galleries. It is without exception the finest illustration of mighty strength in repose that exists. In the days when Glycon the Athenian evolved and produced this masterpiece, art was of more account in the lives of the people than it is now, and so much was his Hercules appreciated and admired that it was impressed on the money of Athens and the coins of Caracalla. Among the many small statuettes that the excavator's shovel has been the means of bringing to light is a very beautiful little winged figure of Victory. Nothing can exceed the grace of the composition and the floating-in-air quality this small treasure possesses. One of the best specimens of Greek bronze work is the so-called Narcissus. A row of bronze statues from the theatre at Pompeii place vividly before one the actors of the Greek stage, just as the armour and magnificent helmets of the gladiators bring the arena and its gory triumphs in front of one's eyes.

But, like the tourist, we must hurry on to the cathedral. The façade, approached by steps from the narrow street, is not in any way noticeable. The interior retains some of the original Gothic, but, owing to earthquakes, has been altered and restored, and now presents itself as a great incongruity to the eye. The illustration will make this apparent. Gothic arches form the bays of the nave. The aisles are also Gothic, and so is the arch over the tribune at the east end. Corinthian shafts and dark marble pilasters run up the square piers of the nave. At the base of the shafts, under classic canopies, are the busts of numerous archbishops, and between the piers are the confessionals. These latter give a rich note of brown, which, with the gilded candelabra on either side of the busts, finds an echo in the heavy and richly coloured ceiling. The vista of the north aisle is the best architectural feature in the building. The south aisle is marred by the obtruding classic columns of its side chapels. At the high altar, which the illustration shows, the blood of S. Januarius liquefies every year on the anniversary of the saint's martyrdom in September. The whole cathedral is then crowded, and the intense fervour and excitement of the immense congregation when the blood, in a phial held aloft by the officiating priest, begins to liquefy, is a sight that once seen can never be forgotten.

Figure 48: INTERIOR OF THE CATHEDRAL, NAPLES

INTERIOR OF THE CATHEDRAL, NAPLES

Immediately under the high altar in the crypt is the Confessio of S. Gennario. Its marble roof is supported by ten Ionic columns. The richly sculptured decoration of the chapel is very fine. The figure of Cardinal Caraffa, who built it, kneels beside the altar under which repose the saint's remains. One other thing of architectural note is the Archbishop's throne in the nave. This good specimen of Gothic work is upheld by most elaborately sculptured pillars, and arches with extremely beautiful tracery.

The most interesting part of Naples lies round the cathedral. Narrow streets, darkened by the clothes that hang from balcony and pole, form a maze which it is easy to wander into, but very difficult to escape from. Some of the finest of the old palaces stand in these dirty thoroughfares. One may pass them a dozen times and still be quite unaware of their existence. The moving crowd that throngs these narrow streets does not show any particular regard for the sightseer, and the careless Jehu who drives whither he will is absolutely unmindful of the pedestrian. So if you would explore old Naples you must look after yourself, and—as a caution too—look after your pockets. It is unwise to display a watch chain, or to carry anything that may be easily snatched from the hand. Remember you are in the midst of expert thieves and among the most heterogeneous race on the face of the globe, a race without the slightest idea of morals of any sort whatever. In the tortuous Via S. Biagio stands a thirteenth-century palace built by one of the Caraffa family, and since known as the Palazzo Santangelo. Some of the best objects in the Museum first found a home in this fine old house. Pope, Paul IV. and the great Neapolitan cardinal, Caraffa, were born in the Palazzo Caraffa in the same street. The central post-office is now housed in the Palazzo Gravina, built in the fifteenth century by one of the Orsini; and the great dwelling of the Monticelli is one of the best specimens of the domestic architecture of the same century.

Not far from the post-office is the church of S. Chiara. Despite the hideous scheme of decoration which has transformed an otherwise fine concert hall—for S. Chiara is more like one than a church—into a curiosity of bad taste, there is a great deal of interest within the fabric. Founded at the commencement of the fourteenth century by Robert the Wise, the church contains his monument and also others of the royal house of Anjou. The frescoes with which Giotto adorned the walls have long ago disappeared, and if it were not for the royal tombs S. Chiara would not be worth a visit. Behind the high altar, at the back of which stairs lead up to a platform enabling one to examine it, is the magnificent tomb of King Robert. The royal sarcophagus rests on Gothic pillars and is adorned by sculptures of the king and his children. His recumbent figure lies extended in the garb of a Franciscan, which Order he entered a few days before his death. Above this, under a canopy, is his figure seated on a throne and clad in royal robes. The beautiful Gothic canopy is supported by slender clustered columns, with five rows of saints in niches carried up to the base of the crocketed pinnacles that surround the canopy. Robert's son Charles, Duke of Calabria, and Mary of Valois, his second wife, lie in sarcophagi that are upheld by figures of angels. These two splendid tombs are to the south of the great king's. To the north are those of Mary, Empress of Constantinople, and of her third husband, Philip of Taranto. Two of her children, Agnese and Clementia, lie also near by; the former, who was married twice, espoused firstly one of the Scaligeri, or della Scala, of Verona. To the right of the high altar is a chapel adorned with fleur-de-lys, the burial place of the royal house of Bourbon. This little chapel and the tombs in it lose greatly in historical sentiment by their hideous and garish surroundings.

S. Domenico Maggiore, the curious exterior of which is illustrated, was originally a noble Gothic edifice. The restorer, unfortunately, has altered and added to this, and although the interior plan is much the same as when first erected, the terrible colours with which it is covered detract in no small measure from its very fine proportions. The sketch shows the exterior of the five-sided apse. The dull yellow tufa with which it is faced and the embattled cornice and buttresses give it a decidedly eastern appearance. S. Domenico may be entered by the door just visible on the left, to reach which one toils up a long flight of moss-grown steps. Push aside the heavy leather flap, and the noisy little piazza, with all Naples beyond, are immediately things of the remote past. You are in a beautiful little twelfth-century chapel. Its walls are lined with most interesting tomb slabs. Note the short figures on each. The Neapolitan is very low of stature, and these short figures, although the tombs are of the twelfth and two succeeding centuries, point to the surmise that the men of the south were never tall. From this chapel one enters the great church at the south transept. Immediately on our left is the sacristy. Here in the gallery which occupies one wall are forty-five burial chests, among which ten hold the remains of ten princes and princesses of the royal line of Aragon. Those which have been identified are Ferdinand I. and II., one of the Dukes of Montalto and his Duchess, and Cardinal Louis d'Aragona. Another contains the husband of the celebrated Vittoria Colonna, the Marquis of Pescara who defeated Francis I. at Pavia. There is something of interest to be found in every chapel in the church. In one of them is the crucifix which conversed with S. Thomas Aquinas while he was composing his *Summa Theologiæ*. The saint's cell may still be seen, and also the room in which he gave his addresses when lecturer in the university that was within the walls of the adjoining monastery. The high altar, raised well above the steps of the choir, is one of the most remarkable specimens of Florentine inlay in the country. It has the curious adjuncts of a recessed seat on either side, and two very fine marble candelabra.

Figure 49: S. DOMENICO MAGGIORE, NAPLES

S. DOMENICO MAGGIORE, NAPLES

These are but three of the three hundred churches Naples possesses. Climb the hill of the Mte Calvari crowned by the Castel Sant' Elmo and look out from the Belvedere in the suppressed Carthusian monastery of S. Martino. Try to count the towers, domes, and spires standing out from the carpet of roofs below. You will be fatigued before you have reached the second hundred. Perhaps the magnificent prospect over the blue bay, with Isola da Capri and the Punta Campanella in the distance, the Sorrentine peninsula and the wonderful shape of Vesuvius on the left, will distract your arithmetic. At any rate the counting of the churches is not worth the trouble when such a glorious view lies before one. Beyond the garden—the old monastic garden, how the monks must have revelled in it!—and beyond the roofs below, the Castel dell' Ovo juts out into the bay. To the left of it, shipping of all nationalities rides the water along the quays near the Arsenal and royal palace. The funnels of huge liners stand up amidst a forest of masts beyond the Immacolatella in a fine sweep to the Rione Margherita di Savoia. Coasting boats with sails like butterflies skim the water. Down in the harbour all is animation; but so far are we above it that not a sound breaks through the distant hum to enable us to distinguish any one particular note.

The cloisters of S. Martino are very beautiful. Sixteen white marble Doric columns form the arcade on each of the four sides. The cells of the departed monks are shut now and the holes through which their food was passed, bricked up. The walls are white; the classic well-head in the centre of the garden is white and so are its steps. The little burial ground in one corner of the court has a white marble balustrade on which are very realistic white marble skulls. Everything gleams white in this quiet court, and the deep blue of the southern sky intensifies it all. For a painter it is a rare study, but perhaps not so fine an one as I once saw years ago. It was in January, snow had fallen for two or three days—even Capri was covered—when with a friend I walked up to the Carthusian monastery of Camaldoli. We reached it just as the fall which had been going on all day ceased. A thick white carpet of fresh untrodden snow lay round us. The white monastery walls looked dull. We rang at the gate, a white garbed monk opened it. We were in a white courtyard surrounded by white walls, and a line of white monks moved slowly towards the chapel. Everything was white. But what a subtlety in the distinction of the colour! Only the sky was grey, and that such a beautiful pearly tone. I question if pigment even in a master's hand could have faithfully reproduced the scene.

Naples was very different in those days. S. Lucia existed then. Now the old harbour is filled up and modern hotels stand where frail wooden piers ran out into the water. From these spider-like structures oysters hung down in baskets fructifying in the outlet of the main sewer! S. Lucia was surpassingly picturesque and gay with the life of the lowest class, but— surpassingly odoriferous. Stalls lined the pavements. Fish of all sorts, cooling drinks, lemons, oranges, every description of fruit, were displayed in the shade of multi-coloured awnings. *Lazzaroni* lay stretched all day long on the sea wall, or slept on the foot-ways propped against the houses. Domestic toilettes performed out of doors in the street never excited remark. And the houses themselves, what a blaze of shifting colour when the wind stirred the sheets and clothing hung out to dry from a hundred balconies! All is changed. The sewage is carried out to sea right away at Cumæ. There are no more oysters at S. Lucia; there is no longer a S. Lucia, but with its disappearance Naples has lost its most unique attraction.

Away at the end of the Chiaia, past the celebrated Marine Aquarium, the hill of Posillipo rises above the little fishing harbour of Mergellina. A tram will carry you swiftly round the corner and along an uphill road from which you will obtain many delightful views. There is nothing on the Riviera to equal the position of some of the fine villas which line this road. Beautiful grounds run down to the sea. Exotic plants grow and flourish, sheltered from the bitter *tramontana* wind. Great pine trees rise solemnly above the tops of their Bay, such as is illustrated, lead one up the steep slopes. Wherever one wanders, it is always the blue sea that is below, and always the wonderful outline of the peninsula across the Bay in the distance or the graceful curves on the flanks of Mount Vesuvius, or, most beautiful of all, the lovely outline of the enchanting Isola da Capri.

Figure 50: THE BAY OF NAPLES FROM POSILLIPO

THE BAY OF NAPLES FROM POSILLIPO

SALERNO

IN the Middle Ages the subject of this chapter was famous throughout Christendom for its school of medicine. S. Thomas Aquinas tells us that in the medical world Salerno ranked where Bologna did in law and Paris in science. Had its fame on this account not been so great, Robert, the son of William the Conqueror, would not have delayed his homeward journey, and stopped there to consult its medical men for a wound he had received in the Holy Land. In consequence of his absence from England, Henry stepped on to the throne which had meanwhile become vacant by the death of Rufus, and the rightful heir never reigned. Salerno was in many other ways connected with the powerful race of Northmen. Robert Guiscard received his mortal wound before the walls of the city as his troops swept over the ramparts at the first assault after an eight months' siege. Roger the Norman was here declared king of Naples and Sicily at a meeting of the barons in 1130, and for many years Salerno was the seat of the Norman government in South Italy. Like many another city which has in the past enjoyed a famous reputation and been of great importance, there is now practically nothing left to tell of its great days. On a crag at the end of the old city walls, some nine hundred feet above the sea, the ruins of the Northmen's stronghold, in the attack on which Robert Guiscard was wounded, still remain, buffeted by the storms that rush up the mountain slopes. The harbour which Manfred commenced to build, and which in old days held the Norman fleet, lies below the Marina, but it silted up many years ago, and is now almost useless for trade. The great days of Salerno have gone, just as the great days of her famous neighbour, Amalfi. The exigencies of modern trade routes and the facilities of the railway have robbed her of all the power and glory she once possessed.

There is, however, something left to remind one of her past wealth and power. Closely hemmed in by its surroundings, the cathedral is not by any means easy to find. Tortuous uphill streets lead to the piazza, where, on a steep incline, a fine double flight of steps with a marble balustrade give on to the spacious cloistered court or atrium beyond which it stands. Robert Guiscard dedicated his cathedral to S. Matteo, and, so that it should be worthy of the great race of de Hauteville, plundered the old Greek city of Pæstum for the building of it. Nearly every one of the pillars of these cloisters came from there. Most of them are so massive that the capitals of native workmanship, probably hewn while the plundering was going on, are too small. The arches above are stilted; they support a gallery whereon a row of statues of different archbishops appear in a now much delapidated condition. The same state of partial ruin greets the eye as one looks around. Fourteen ancient sarcophagi, nearly all of them Greek, stand in the cloisters of the court. They were used by the Normans for Christian burial, but, alas! are mutilated and chipped at the corners, and their fine bas-reliefs, one of a hunting scene, another with centaurs and nymphs on the panels, are almost completely ruined by the ill-treatment they have received. In the centre of the court is a fountain. Water still splashes in its Greek basin, but decay and neglect have robbed this otherwise beautiful atrium of most of its charm.

The cathedral adjoins the courtyard. The bronze doors of the central porch were at one time inlaid with silver. The precious metal has disappeared, but small figures of the Apostles and Christian symbols bear evidence that when these doors came fresh from Constantinople in the eleventh century they were of very fine craftsmanship. The interior of the great church is whitewashed. The floor slopes up towards the east end, and is a good example of a well arranged marble pattern. The most interesting things, if we except the tombs that are in the building, are the two *ambones*, or pulpits. That which appears in the illustration is a wonderful example of the work of John of Procida. The other, as well as the archbishop's throne, is by the same great designer. All three are masterpieces of the Græco-Byzantine style of inlaid *tesseræ*. In the illustration will be seen a fine Paschal candelabrum, with most intricate inlay, as fine in its way as that described in the next chapter. These pulpits are approached by steps from inside the choir. One is supported by four columns of rare porphyry and the other by twelve of granite from Pæstum. Age has toned the white marble panels to a light grey, which gives a wonderfully fine note to the white of the cathedral walls as one looks up the nave from the west end. The choir is encircled with a most beautiful inlaid marble screen, in decoration similar to the two pulpits. The floor is a grand example of *opus Alexandrinum* inlay, and is as good in this respect as the best in Italy.

Figure 51: A PULPIT IN THE CATHEDRAL, SALERNO

A PULPIT IN THE CATHEDRAL, SALERNO

Under the high altar, in the crypt, is a monument to S. Matthew, with a seated bronze figure of the saint. Below this, in a casket, repose the remains of the Evangelist, which were brought here in the year 930. The crypt itself is not interesting. To find what is, we must return to the church above, where some of the tombs are well worthy of study. Pope Gregory VII., Hildebrand, who died in Salerno, lies in a sarcophagus in one of the side chapels. The remains of Margaret of Anjou, mother of King Ladislaus, rest under the canopy of a fine tomb, on which in relief the queen is depicted surrounded by her children and her maids of honour. Angels form the support to the canopy, which is decorated with gold fleur-de-lys on a blue ground. Archbishop Caraffa's remains are in a fine Greek sarcophagus with Medusa heads at its corners. On another is a fine bas-relief of the Triumph of Bacchus, and many more, like those in the cloisters, have been transferred from Pagan use to Christian. The chapel in which is Hildebrand's tomb belongs to the family of John of Precida, who decorated it himself.

In the sacristy is a very interesting *Palla* of ivory, the thirty panels of which represent scenes in the Old and New Testaments. This eleventh-century work is one of the few things which can with truth be said to be in excellent preservation. The cathedral, like its surroundings, is sadly in need of repair. Its fine *campanile* is buttressed up, or would long ago have toppled into the street below. The two lowest storeys of this grand tower are the original Norman work of Roger's day. At their angles are marble and granite columns, no doubt from Pæstum. The two upper storeys are not like the lower, built of stone, but have been constructed in a very beautifully coloured brick. They are pierced by Norman arches, above which is the belfry surmounted by a dome. Were it not for the few things we have noted, Salerno would not be worth a visit. But if only to see the magnificent pulpits and stand silently in the crypt by the remains of the Evangelist, the tourist in his hurry should never omit to spend at least a few hours in this once famous city.

PALERMO

PHŒNICIANS, Carthaginians, Greeks and Romans, Goths, Byzantines, Normans and Spaniards, have all ruled in Sicily; and those whose curiosity takes them to the museum of Palermo may there see many antiquities of great interest in the history of each period. The man who observes may also see much in her streets. There are distinct quarters in Palermo where the different races and their descendants have kept themselves to themselves from time immemorial. It takes no special knowledge of racial physiognomy to single out among other types the Berber or the Greek, as one saunters along watching the ever-changing crowd in the lively thoroughfares. The Norman occupation is recalled in the vivid decoration of the panels of the peasants' carts. On them one sees the gallant Norman slaying the truculent Infidel— slaying them by dozens! Quite archaic is the execution of these panels—the handiwork of a long line of painters, whose progenitors hundreds of years ago were painting the same scenes on the vehicles of their day. The colours are crude. Every inch of the car is painted. The spokes of the wheels are notched and carved. The body of the cart is firmly fixed, high above the axle bar, by well-arranged ironwork of floral design. There are no other carts in existence like them; and when the feathered plume of ultramarine and red which always adorns the donkey's headgear, and the tinselled harness worked with gold and silver thread, are new, not many chariots or state coaches make a braver show.

Palermo is divided into four quarters by the two streets that, running east and west, north and south, bisect one another at the circular space in the centre of the city called the Quattro Canti—the Four Corners. Standing in this busy spot and looking downhill northwards, the deep blue of the Mediterranean bounds the horizon. South the view is partially stopped by the great city gateway, the arch of the Porta Nuova which crosses the street by the Royal Palace nearly a mile away. East and west, high over the heads of the crowd and the congested traffic, grand mountains rise up with a puff of white cloud above their summits. In whichever direction one gazes the vista ends, far beyond the lines of tall houses, with the blue sea or the blue sky.

169

Figure 52: THE CATHEDRAL. PALERMO

THE CATHEDRAL. PALERMO

If one walks towards the Royal Palace up the hill, one passes through the fine Piazza del Duomo. It is a large square enclosed on three sides by a marble balustrade, on which stand, at intervals, colossal statues of bishops and saints. On the fourth side is the great cathedral. This fine specimen of pointed Sicilian work is dedicated to S. Maria Assunta, and was commenced in the twelfth century when Gualterio Offamilio, Walter of the Mill, was the English archbishop of Palermo. The curious architectural style of the building is due to the fact that it was designed by a Norman and carried out by Moorish workmen. The Moor found it impossible to leave out his native arcades and his battlements; and the diaper pattern on the west façade recalls in design the decoration of the east. The Saracenic capitals of the beautifully carved pillars of the three doors of this façade are exceptionally good. Norman zig-zag moulding embellishes the arches above. Niches filled with saints add to the harmonious incongruity so subtly arranged by infidel workmen. A noble tower at each corner rises in eight tiers, the three topmost being open.

Throughout these towers small arches are supported by little marble columns with their corners rounded off in a bold way by ringed pillars. They terminate in little turrets and pinnacles, which have flames at their bases. To break all the flat surfaces of these, the Eastern mind was constrained to put some sort of decoration, thus carrying off the appearance of great weightiness; and so, square, billet, lozenge, and nail-head patterns have been most admirably introduced. The lower portion of the great tower across the street and opposite the façade, and which forms part of the archbishop's palace, is Saracenic, and was erected before the Northman's advent in Sicily. The upper stages are the belfry. Despite the spires which all these towers possess, there is something decidedly more Eastern than Northern in their appearance. The arches that cross the street—so bold a feature in the sketch—were put up in the twelfth century to sustain the palace and cathedral whenever earthquake shocks occurred.

The cathedral is entered by the south porch. This is flanked by twelfth-century towers, on the top of which are ugly white marble figures, executed at a bad period. Three stilted arches of Moorish design with cable mouldings, the central arch larger than the other two, support a rather low gable. The face of this gable is covered with a good scheme of decoration. The cornice is deeply cut with animals and foliage, a porcupine and a hare being among the former. Four grotesque Norman waterspouts break the string course between the cornice and a beautiful flat arcade under the arches, on which are half-length figures of saints and bishops. The wall beneath this and above the three arches of the porch was evidently at one time covered with Arab designs in black and red. Four grey marble pillars with their eastern capitals support the arches; they came from the mosque which stood on the spot where the cathedral was erected. The portal of the door itself is a real masterpiece of intricate Moorish carving. Here pomegranates and palm leaves occupy a prominent place. In the eighteenth century many alterations occurred, and this grand and, from an architectural point of view, deeply interesting church, was disfigured to a large extent. The porch has suffered almost as much as the interior of the building. But one tablet worth recording still exists in the former:

PRIM . SEDES . CORONA . REGIS . ET . REGNI . CAPUT

Thus runs the proud title of the city in the days when the kings of Sicily were crowned in Palermo's cathedral. A row of white marble figures stands on the exterior of the side chapels of the aisles. They are bad. Little domes with glazed tiles also remind one of a later period. These, with the big central dome over the crossing, were the work of Fuga, a Neapolitan architect. In the alterations he carried out, the battlements and the corbel tables under them were spared. The latter are a very curious study in the physiognomy of the different races known to the Normans when the cathedral was built. Executed by Arab workmen, whose faith forbade them to portray the handiwork of Allah, their accuracy is not unimpeachable. The east end is partly covered with flat arcading, most elaborately carved with Arabic design, and partly with a black and red pattern of the same character. The apse is not pierced by any lights.

The white-washed classic interior is a great disappointment after the rich brown and yellow stone of the exterior. But if, architecturally, it fails to interest, historically it is concerned with the most brilliant and prosperous period the city enjoyed. Turning to the left on entering the cathedral by the south porch are the two chapels wherein stand in solemn grandeur the mighty sarcophagi of the Norman and Swabian kings. The remains of Roger, the first Norman ruler of Sicily, rest in a porphyry sarcophagus supported by marble feet composed of four crouching Saracens. The fine canopy above is incrusted with mosaic. Its pillars are gilded and inlaid. The next tomb is that of Constantia, who was the last of the royal line of Normans. She was the wife of the Emperor Henry VI., and mother of Frederick II. By the side of this is the sarcophagus of Henry VI. Very elaborately adorned is that which contains the remains of Frederick II., and the body of Peter II. of Aragon. The lid of this is carved with medallions of Christ, and the Virgin and child. All that is left of Constance, wife of Frederick II., is in a Roman sarcophagus which is recessed in a wall of the chapel. It is beautifully decorated with a hunting scene in bas-relief. Standing against another wall is a mediæval tomb, with a cowled figure between two shields, on which are displayed the eagles of Aragon. It holds the ashes of William, Duke of Athens, who was a son of Frederick of Aragon. All these tombs are not only full of archæological interest in themselves, but when one reviews the origin and history of the Norman occupation of the island, the chapel in which they rest becomes one of the most historically absorbing spots in the world.

The Saracens were in possession of Sicily when Roger, the youngest of the twelve sons of Tancred de Hauteville, came over from Apulia, where his brothers, by force of arms, had established themselves as reigning Counts. Roger found all the civilisation, culture, and well-ordered bureaucracy of the Moor firmly established. And with this he was too wise to interfere. Changing nothing of the mode of life of those he conquered, but simply adding to it the strength of arm and vitality of a northern race, he became—and those who followed him were—by far the richest and most magnificent sovereigns of their time in all Europe.

The crypt is architecturally the most interesting part of the interior of the cathedral. It contains the tombs of twenty-four of Palermo's archbishops, including that of Walter of the Mill. Among the treasures in the sacristy is the cap of Constance of Aragon, which was found in her tomb, when, by order of Ferdinand I., the royal sarcophagi were opened. On one of the rough gems with which the cap is studded, is written in Arabic, "In Christ, God, I put my hope." Here, again, is evidence that the Moor and Christian lived amicably side by side. Theodoric in Ravenna, and the Norman in Palermo, brought peace to the land they conquered; and the greatest prosperity that both cities enjoyed was a consequence of their wisdom, and of their religious tolerance.

In the fine open square which one reaches at the end of the seemingly interminable Corso, a Roman house and other very interesting remains are now being unearthed. The Royal Palace occupies one side of the piazza, and, being the highest part of the city, is on the site of the old Roman palace. There is a magnificent view from the observatory situated on the roof of the building. It is, however, with the beautiful chapel built by Roger II. in the early part of the twelfth century that we are concerned. The Cappella Palatina is a perfect gem, and no one who has once visited it in the morning can ever forget the marvellous effect of dim light passing through its narrow windows, and illuminating its wonderful marble and mosaic walls. Three of the bays of the nave are formed by columns of Egyptian granite which alternate with three of fluted Greek marble. The composite capitals of the arches are Byzantine and Corinthian. These arches are stilted and covered in an extremely rich manner with gorgeous mosaic, and their soffits inlaid with *tesseræ* arranged in Moorish designs. The walls of the aisles are lined with the richest marble slabs, beneath which a beautiful dado of inlaid Eastern pattern runs round the chapel. The wooden roof of the nave is honeycombed, and like that of the Alhambra at Granada is arranged with splendidly coloured and gilded pendentives. Cufic inscriptions find a place amongst these hanging clusters. The ceilings of the aisles are coffered and sustain heavy gold bosses, which enrich the gorgeous effect of their strong colour.

The choir is raised five steps above the nave, from which it is shut off by a very beautiful marble screen. The stalls are carved perpendicular work. The fine wooden lectern of very late Gothic design has well-carved angels kneeling on the four supporting legs. Above these angels four kings stand around the centre column. On the book-rest repose the old black-letter parchment psalters. At the top of all, the Virgin and Child finish off this exceedingly well-designed and executed reading-desk. Beyond the choir the apse rises four steps. The risers of these steps and those of the choir are most beautifully inlaid. The colossal mosaic figure in the semi-dome of the apse is the only mosaic of a late date; and, aiming at the qualities of a painting, like those on the exterior of S. Mark's and the cathedral at Orvieto, somewhat mars the uniformity and simplicity of the *tesseræ* decoration of the chapel. The floor of the building is entirely *opus Alexandrinum*. At the west end, a raised dais for the exclusive use of royalty is railed off, and a portrait of the reigning sovereign let into the marble panels of the wall. By the pulpit stands a Byzantine candelabrum. Four lions rending their prey are at its base. Other animals and birds and figures of men, all fighting one another, encircle, in orderly confusion, the beautiful inlaid central column. Above them is a figure of the Almighty, serenely quiescent. Children, symbolical of innocence and freedom from sin, are carved round the bowl into which is stuck the huge Easter candle. It is very difficult to describe the effect of sudden calm that steals over one when, entering this dark church, with the glare of the sun and the noise of the streets outside, one is conscious of a very restful gloom, full of the richest colour, and a silence soothing to the senses. One somehow feels the gorgeousness of the east combined with the solemnity of a well-planned sacred interior, and this despite the sudden transition from light to darkness. There is no other building of like dimensions which grips one as does the wonderful Cappella Palatina of Palermo.

La Martorana, away down in the city, may have been as beautiful, but unfortunately in the year 1590 the nuns of the attached convent ordered most of the precious mosaics to be stripped from the walls, and a hideous choir added when these were demolished. Some few are left on the roof to tell us what a glorious thing this finely proportioned chapel must have been before religious zeal got the better of artistic taste. The central apse was likewise taken down a hundred years later, and with it more priceless mosaic destroyed. The inlaid marble on the walls was done away with in the eighteenth century. If anything better could have been found to take the place of the grand mosaics that covered the interior there might have been an excuse for these acts of vandalism but when one sees the hideous stucco and wretched mural paintings of bad design and colour, that have no religious fervour or tendency and nothing whatever to recommend them in any way, one stands aghast at the ignorance and stupidity which in the name of religious expediency destroyed such priceless treasures. Among the little that remains are two curious mosaics wherein King Roger is crowned by Christ, and the High Admiral, who founded the church, is dedicating it to the Virgin. The king is wearing the dalmatic. This he received, together with the mitre, from the Pope, who found it more diplomatic to confer ecclesiastical office upon the Norman king than to oppose him in useless wars.

A little to the south of the Royal Palace, and almost abutting on the old walls of the city, is S. Giovanni degli Eremiti. The beautiful cloistered garden, which is adjacent, forms an illustration to this chapter. The little church is a very early specimen of Norman work on the plan of the letter T with three apses. On its south side is a tiny mosque, incorporated with the building and utilised in the old days as a chapel. The monastery, which existed here in the time of Gregory the Great, had fallen into disuse when the Normans came to Sicily, and King Roger restored the old buildings. The interior now is absolutely bare and the windows unglazed. The Moorish domes give the little church a very eastern appearance, to which the flat members of the rustic stones of the cloister arches in no small measure add. It is a peaceful spot where exotic plants flourish luxuriantly, and vie with all sorts of flowers in wanton growth.

Figure 53: THE CLOISTERS OF S. GIOVANNI DEGLI EREMITI, PALERMO

THE CLOISTERS OF S. GIOVANNI DEGLI EREMITI, PALERMO

The traveller who has been in Spain will find in the old quarter of Palermo many palaces that will remind him of Seville, Salamanca, and other places in the Iberian peninsula. The tawny colour of the South predominates here, and the two or three courtyards possessed by many of these palaces will add to his reminiscences. This is not so strange as it may seem when one considers that from the year 1282, when Pedro of Aragon was crowned king, to 1713, when Victor Amadeus, Duke of Savoy, ascended the throne, Sicily was under the rule of the Spaniard. The great square block of yellow stone in the Piazza Marina, the Palazzo Chiaramonte, served as the palace of the Spanish Viceroys and headquarters of the Inquisition. Now known as the Palazzo de' Tribunali, it is used as the law courts. The ante-chamber of the court room has a magnificent wooden ceiling. Hunting about in the narrow streets in this quarter one chances on many a piece of architecture and decorative sculpture in the grandiose style of the great days of Spain. One or two good fountains and fine portals add much to the historical charm of a part of the city which is now occupied by humble folk. The church of S. Agostino, difficult to find in the slums, has a remarkable façade with a beautiful wheel window. Delicate white marble pillars radiate from the Paschal Lamb, which is the hub of the wheel, and three rows of tiny but beautifully-carved arches interlace and form the tracery of the window. The chevroned arches of the portal are decorated with acanthus leaves and arabesques. The capitals of the supporting columns are pomegranates, and a flat canopy with dripstone of acanthus leaves, beneath which are almost obliterated frescoes, completes one of the most fascinating relics of bygone days to be found anywhere in Palermo. It is in the old quarters, too, that the life of the *cittadini* is seen in its most picturesque garb. Fruit shops, full of golden oranges and pale lemons, prickly pears and great citrons, make gay patches of colour in the street vista. Glazed tiles, earthenware, and vividly coloured cotton goods displayed outside the shop fronts or hanging from the walls add to the variety of the scene. Cookshops, with *pizzi* and *scaglozzi*, and olive oil in the frying pan, excite the olfactory nerves in a pleasanter degree than those in which a particularly strong-flavoured cheese finds ready purchasers. Excellent wine may be drunk at a very small cost at the drinking bars, where a jet of clear water is for ever playing over the marble slabs of the cistern-like counter. Fowls scurry about in the midst of the throng, and hungry dogs scent a meal in the refuse heaps of the gutters. All is animation, and all has a touch of the South that is something more than Italian. It is almost worth while going to Palermo in order to perambulate her fascinating streets and observe the ever-changing crowd that peoples them.

Figure 54: MTE. PELLIGRINO, PALERMO

MTE. PELLIGRINO, PALERMO

It is certainly worth the voyage to enter the harbour when the sun is well up and from the ship's deck watch the splendid panorama unfold itself as the vessel glides into port. At the foot of Mte Pelligrino, and where the famous valley of the Conca d'Oro, or Golden Shell, touches the blue waters of the Mediterranean, lies Palermo. Beyond, with an inclination upwards to the lower slopes of Mte Cuccio in the distance, stretches the triangular shaped valley, Mte Cuccio forming the apex of the triangle. Mountains hem the landscape in on two sides. The whole of the country between them and the sea is one vast grove of orange and lemon trees. On the edge of the receding wall of mountains to the right of the valley in the middle distance, a stately building stands above the brow of a steep hill. Round it cluster roofs and walls in irregular lines. This is Monreale. To Monreale we go to study the mosaics. For though its cathedral boasts of grand twelfth-century bronze doors, and a very fine portico, the magnificent mosaics that cover the walls of the interior are its pride and glory.

The decoration of this fine basilica may be described as a coherent mass of superb mosaics and well selected slabs of grey and white marble inlaid with panels of Moorish design. Here more than in any other church in the world has architecture been subordinated to a scheme of gorgeously coloured decoration. Its Mosaics are Greek in style, with Greek inscriptions. Moorish designs and arabesques also rival in colour the extraordinarily intricate gold pattern which sets off the beauty of the marble walls. On the semi-dome of the central apse is a very impressive colossal half-length mosaic of the Saviour holding an open book. Below, are figures of the archangels, Gabriel and Michael, and the twelve apostles. The vault of the south apse contains a gigantic figure of S. Peter, and in the corresponding one in the north apse, one of S. Paul. These two figures are robed in white, and light up the dark recesses of the deep-toned gold background of the apses in a remarkable manner. In the choir there is a mosaic over the royal throne very similar to that in La Martorana, wherein King Roger is being crowned. In this case Christ places the crown on the head of William the Good. Over the Archbishop's throne William is represented offering the church to the Virgin. Sicily was never a fief of the Popes, and these two mosaics no doubt express the idea that the sovereigns derived their authority from God alone.

Round the whole of the nave two sets or series of mosaics are arranged which, beginning at the Flood, illustrate different episodes in biblical history. Forty-two scenes are depicted in the nave and ten in each aisle which deal with our Lord's life as well as themes from the Old Testament. At the west end is a mosaic of S. Castrense, Monreale's tutelar saint, casting out a devil, and also walking on the sea.

Comparing these wonderful decorations with those at Ravenna and in S. Mark's, one may at first be more impressed with the apparent magnificence of the scheme which we find here. The cathedral is larger than any of Ravenna's churches, and has this advantage over S. Mark's, that one is better able here to grasp at once the whole idea of the colour scheme. In S. Mark's one sits and quietly discovers things at leisure. At Monreale one enters and is immediately overpowered by the magnificence of the dull gold *tesseræ* and the gorgeous arrangement of the sequence of figures which, like a flash, strike one at first sight. Ravenna can show us better schemes of colour, subtler and more refined. Ravenna gives us earlier work, and work more naïve, and is for this reason more attractive and interesting. But it must be admitted that in no other building of the kind is one impelled to stop suddenly and catch one's breath, as when first entering Monreale's great basilica.

Eight bays divide the nave from the aisles. Their stilted arches are supported by granite monoliths. The capitals of these are pure Corinthian, and Corinthian with cornucopiæ volutes and medallion heads. Above the abacus of each capital is the simple Norman bowl capital inlaid with rich mosaic. It is from these that the glorious colour-scheme springs—above and around, the eye finds nothing but mosaic. The lower portion of the walls of the aisles is composed of marble slabs separated from one another by inlay of Moorish design. In the north chancel aisle are the tombs of Roger, Duke of Apulia, and Henry, Prince of Capua, two sons of William the Bad. In the south chancel aisle are the tombs of William the Good and William II. Just as Palermo's cathedral is a fit resting-place for the remains of some of the Norman kings, so is this grand fabric for the bodies of those of the same royal line who here repose in peace.

Figure 55: THE CLOISTERS, MONREALE

THE CLOISTERS, MONREALE

Adjoining the cathedral, on the south side, is all that is left of the original Benedictine monastery. The celebrated cloisters, of which we speak, are more Arab than Norman, and more infidel than Christian in their architecture. The two flat members of the Moorish arches are decorated with black *tufa* lozenges and spearheads. The coupled columns are nowhere approached in beauty and delicacy, save in S. Paolo fuori at Rome. Arabesques cover some of them; all were at one time richly inlaid with mosaic. Some are chevroned, others of lozenge pattern, or billeted, or twisted and spiral. Their capitals are one and all of extreme interest. One shows on its carved surface Norman knights in chain mail engaged in combat with Saracens; another, Roman gladiators slaying Christian victims. Birds, beasts, and subjects from the Old Testament, intricate foliage and vines add to a variety which is not to be found anywhere else in the cloistered courts of Italy. The illustration gives a corner of this beautiful spot where a fountain splashes and plays, adding to the delights of a well-kept garden and the sweet scent of flowers.

INDEX: A, B, C, D, E, F, G, H, J, K, L, M, N, O, P, Q, R, S, T, U, V, W, Z

Zuccaro, 188

PRINTED BY
BALLANTYNE & COMPANY LTD
TAVISTOCK STREET COVENT GARDEN
LONDON